# The Prayer Jar

### DEVOTIONAL

## FORGIVENESS

# The Prayer Jar

## D E V O T I O N A L

## FORGIVENESS

# WANDA E. BRUNSTETTER

*with*

## DONNA K. MALTESE

## BARBOUR

P U B L I S H I N G

Print ISBN 978-1-63609-637-7

Cover Design: Greg Jackson, Thinkpen Design

Published by Barbour Publishing, Inc., 1810 Barbour Drive, Uhrichsville, Ohio 44683, www.barbourbooks.com

*Our mission is to inspire the world with the life-changing message of the Bible.*

Member of the
Evangelical Christian
Publishers Association

Printed in China.

# FORGIVENESS

Webster's Dictionary defines the word *forgive* as "to grant pardon for or to." God's Word teaches us that forgiveness is the act of pardoning an offender. The Greek word translated *forgiveness* means "to let go," as when a person does not demand payment for a debt. Jesus used this comparison when He taught His followers to pray: "And forgive us our sins; for we also forgive every one that is indebted to us" (Luke 11:4 KJV). In another passage of scripture, Jesus compared forgiveness to canceling a debt (Matthew 18:23-35).

In my novel, *The Forgiving Jar,* the main character, Sara, had to reach the point where she could forgive her deceased mother for not telling the truth about her Amish heritage and the parents who had raised her. She also needed to forgive Michelle, who in Book 1, *The Hope Jar,* fooled Sara's Amish grandparents by pretending to be Sara.

It is my hope and prayer that this devotional book will help you, the reader, to fully understand the true meaning of forgiveness. Emotional healing begins when we choose to forgive. And when God forgives us, our sins are washed away.

> *For if ye forgive men their trespasses,*
> *your heavenly Father will also forgive you.*
> MATTHEW 6:14 KJV

# What Is A Prayer Jar?

One of the most important things we can do to help forgiveness flourish in our lives is to pray. James 4:8 tells us that if we want to draw closer to God, we must reach out to Him. By going to God in prayer, we're able to offer our adoration, petitions, intercessions, and thanks to Him. One way we can remind ourselves to pray often is to make a prayer jar and place it where we will see it every day. Each time we look at the jar, we'll think of someone or something for which we want to pray. A prayer jar can strengthen our faith and deepen our relationship with God.

A prayer jar can be something as simple as a canning jar. It can be plain or decorated with ribbons, stickers, buttons, sequins, feathers, or glitter. The one I use is a plain antique canning jar. I write my prayer requests, scripture verses, and notes of thanks to God on small strips of paper. After praying about the request or reflecting on the Bible verse, I fold the paper in half and place it in the prayer jar. From time to time, I take out one or more of the prayers—and if that particular prayer has been answered, I thank the Lord and then write down the date. If my prayer request has not yet been answered, it goes back into the jar.

Do you have a special prayer request today? If so, consider creating your own prayer jar.

# FORGIVENESS FROM GOD

Have you ever wondered how and why God can forgive sins—especially the most terrible ones by our standards? Big or small, our sins separate us from God, yet all we have to do is repent.

God forgives us because we need forgiveness. "And I will cleanse them from all their iniquity, whereby they have sinned against me; and I will pardon all their iniquities, whereby they have sinned, and whereby they have transgressed against me" (Jeremiah 33:8 KJV).

God forgives because He is merciful and wants to see our comfort. "Blessed be God, even the Father of our Lord Jesus Christ, the Father of mercies, and the God of all comfort" (2 Corinthians 1:3 KJV).

God forgives us because He desires to take our worries away. "Cast thy burden upon the LORD, and he shall sustain thee: he shall never suffer the righteous to be moved" (Psalm 55:22 KJV).

Isn't it wonderful to know that our Heavenly Father loves us so much that He provided a way—through the shedding of Christ's blood—for our sins to be forgiven? The best part is that our forgiveness is only a prayer away.

# SIN MAKES ITS ENTRANCE: PART 1

*Do not love the world or the things that belong to the world. . . . For everything that belongs to the world—the lust of the flesh, the lust of the eyes, and the pride in one's lifestyle—is not from the Father, but is from the world.*

1 JOHN 2:15-16 HCSB

Without sin, we wouldn't need forgiveness. So before we dive into the latter, we need to spend some time looking at the former.

Sin first entered the world in the beginning, specifically Genesis 3. God set the scene in Genesis 1-2, where He created the heavens and earth, flora and fauna, sea and creatures, man and woman. The humans were in the garden of Eden, happily living in communion with their Creator. Enter the serpent, God's craftiest creature. He began to test the godly couple by getting Eve alone and questioning her about God's instructions. In his own sly way, the father of lies started twisting God's words.

Having taught Eve how to doubt God's commands, the serpent convinced her to eat of the tree of knowledge of good and evil. With one bite, the holiness of God's creation was broken.

*Lord, may I love You and Your words more than anything the world offers.*

## PRAYER JAR INSPIRATION:

*With Your help, Lord, may I resist temptation.*

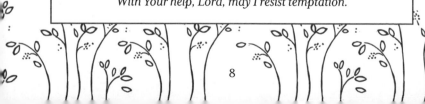

# SIN MAKES ITS ENTRANCE: PART 2

*When the woman saw that the tree was good for food, and that it was pleasant to the eyes, and a tree to be desired to make one wise, she took of the fruit thereof, and did eat, and gave also unto her husband with her; and he did eat. And the eyes of them both were opened, and they knew that they were naked.*

GENESIS 3:6-7 KJV

Having taken a bite of the forbidden fruit, Eve offered it to Adam. He, too, rebelled against God by eating from the luscious fruit. Now their eyes were opened to a new reality. They realized they were naked, and that fact filled them with shame. So, they sewed some fig leaves together to cover themselves.

Soon, the hapless couple realized that God was walking in the garden. Embarrassed and guilt-ridden, Adam and Eve hid themselves from His presence. But when God called out to Adam, asking where he was, the first man made the first confession: "I heard the sound of You [walking] in the garden, and I was afraid because I was naked; and I hid myself" (Genesis 3:10 AMPC). And in that moment, the ugly truth was revealed.

*Lord, may I never hide anything from You, including myself.*

## PRAYER JAR INSPIRATION:
*Give me the courage, God, to always come clean to You.*

# THE BLAME GAME

*He asked, "Who told you that you were naked? Did you eat from the tree that I commanded you not to eat from?" Then the man replied, "The woman You gave to be with me—she gave me some fruit from the tree, and I ate." . . . And the woman said, "It was the serpent. He deceived me, and I ate."*

GENESIS 3:11–13 HCSB

Sin had entered paradise. Now shame, fear, and blame followed close behind.

God's children were hiding from Him. He knew they'd learned to deny His words, that they'd disobeyed His one command by eating fruit from the forbidden tree. Having obtained the knowledge of good and evil, they realized they were naked and felt ashamed. Now in hiding, the couple heard God walking around in the garden and looking for them. Suddenly, fear made its first appearance.

When God asked them how this happened, Adam blamed God for giving him his companion, Eve, who'd given him the fruit. Eve blamed the serpent who'd tricked her into eating the forbidden food.

Yet, ultimately, each individual has no one to blame but oneself when tempted into sin. And each needs forgiveness from God.

*When I sin, Lord, may I not play the blame game but admit it was I who erred.*

## PRAYER JAR INSPIRATION:

*Lord, this was my fault. . .*

# CONSEQUENCES

*The L*ORD* God said to the serpent, "Because you have done this,*
*you are cursed. . . ." Then he said to the woman, "I will sharpen*
*the pain of your pregnancy. . . ." And to the man he said, "Since*
*you listened to your wife and ate from the tree whose fruit I*
*commanded you not to eat, the ground is cursed because of you."*
GENESIS 3:14, 16, 17 NLT

In response to the misdeeds of the serpent, the woman, and the man, God laid out the consequences for their actions.

The serpent was fated to forever crawl on its belly, to grovel in the dust, to continually endure hostility between it and the woman and her offspring. The woman would have greater pain in labor and would desire her husband, who'd be the dominant partner in their relationship. The man would have to toil for every bit of food he received from the earth. Worst of all, God told Adam, "You [will] return to the ground from which you were made. For you were made from dust, and to dust you will return" (Genesis 3:19 NLT).

God makes it clear that our misdeeds, even after they're forgiven, will still have consequences. But fortunately for us, Jesus will transform the results of our sins. As F. B. Meyers wrote, "Where sin abounded, grace abounds much more."

*I look toward Your grace, Lord, to help me bear*
*the consequences of my missteps.*

## PRAYER JAR INSPIRATION:
*God's grace abounds!*

11

# COVERED BY GOD

*The L&#x1d0f;RD God made clothing out of skins for Adam*
*and his wife, and He clothed them.*

GENESIS 3:21 HCSB

Despite Adam and Eve's disobedience, God still showed them His love and care. In doing so, He revealed His forgiving nature. To protect His children from the heat and cold, God killed some animals and used their skins to tenderly cover the humans' nakedness. Perhaps the animal skins would remind His children of their fall into sin.

In their nakedness, Adam and Eve had been innocent and honorable. Now, to cover their shame and allay their fears, death entered paradise.

This killing to cover the couple's sins foreshadowed what Jesus would one day do to cover ours. Adam and Eve's fig leaves were not an adequate covering. But in His grace, mercy, love, and kindness, God made the pair long and durable coats of skin to protect them from the elements. This reminds us that God provides forgiveness for deeds past, present, and future.

*Thank You, Lord, for always taking such good care of me—for Your love, gentleness, mercy, grace, and kindness. You alone allay my fears. You alone wipe away my tears. To You alone I sing my praise!*

---

## PRAYER JAR INSPIRATION:

*Thank You, God, for always being there for me.*

---

# OUT OF THE GARDEN

*Then the L*ORD *God said, "Look, the human beings have become like us, knowing both good and evil. What if they reach out, take fruit from the tree of life, and eat it? Then they will live forever!"*

GENESIS 3:22 NLT

Man, who'd been made in the image of God, had lost his innocence. Because of his disobedience to God's command, he was now familiar with both good and evil. The present danger lay in creatures of man's ilk living forever.

Thus, the three-in-one God, the Holy Trio, the "us" referred to in Genesis 3:22, decided Adam and Eve must now vacate paradise. Although forgiven by God, the sinful creatures were driven out of the Garden of Eden to make their way in the outer world. The price of their missteps would be death. Their way back to God would eventually lie in the hands of a Redeemer who would willingly take their punishment.

This is how Genesis 3 ends: "After driving them out, [God] stationed winged guardians at the east end of the garden of Eden and set up a sword of flames which alertly turned back and forth to guard the way to the tree of life" (verse 24 VOICE). The individual who'd once been given the task to "tend and guard and keep" (Genesis 2:15 AMPC) the garden would now be guarded from it.

*Thank You, Jesus, for redeeming me from sin and giving me eternal life.*

## PRAYER JAR INSPIRATION:

*Jesus is my way back into Paradise.*

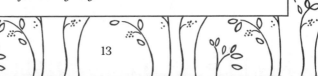

# A COMPASSIONATE GOD

*Then the L*ord *passed in front of him and proclaimed: Yahweh—*
*Yahweh is a compassionate and gracious God, slow to anger*
*and rich in faithful love and truth, maintaining faithful love*
*to a thousand generations, forgiving wrongdoing, rebellion,*
*and sin. But He will not leave the guilty unpunished.*

Exodus 34:6-7 hcsb

God's love is lavish. Time and time again, we make mistakes, we revolt and rebel, we deviate from where He wants us to go and from what He wants us to be. Yet, our Lord still keeps loving His creation. Why? Because He is filled with compassion for us—even when we are coldhearted.

Thankfully, God is slow to get angry. He is faithful with His love. He always speaks the truth. And He forgives whenever we stray.

How do we know that God has all these wonderful attitudes toward fault-ridden females such as us? Because He allowed His one and only Son to die to cover our sins so that we could be close to Him again.

Today, bask in the truth of who God was, is, and always will be: "a compassionate and gracious God, slow to anger and rich in faithful love and truth, maintaining faithful love to a thousand generations, forgiving wrongdoing, rebellion, and sin."

*Thank You, Lord, for having compassion on me.*

## PRAYER JAR INSPIRATION:

*Yahweh is my compassionate and gracious God!*

# READY TO FORGIVE

*For You, O Lord, are good, and ready to forgive [our trespasses, sending them away, letting them go completely and forever]; and You are abundant in mercy and loving-kindness to all those who call upon You.*

PSALM 86:5 AMPC

Make no mistake: you belong to a God who is ready to forgive.

In Psalm 86, David begins by asking God to listen to him—to hear his words and answer his prayer. He describes himself as "poor and distressed, needy and desiring" (Psalm 86:1 AMPC) and reminds God he's faithful to Him (verse 2). David then appeals to God's mercy, explaining he has been crying to Him and calling on Him constantly (verse 3). David wants to rejoice as he lifts his soul up to the only One who can grant him the forgiveness he so desperately desires. He knows that God, out of the goodness of His heart and out of His abundant mercy and love, is ready, willing, and able to forgive.

You, like David, have the same assurance: when you come to God, He will be ready to forgive. You can be certain that when troubles come knocking, God will answer you (verse 7). Why? Because our incomparable God stands alone and above all others (verse 8)!

*O Lord, my God, I come with a heavy heart,*
*knowing You are ready to forgive.*

## PRAYER JAR INSPIRATION:

*My God is always ready to forgive.*

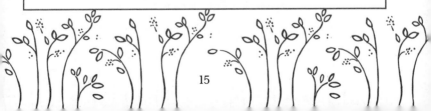

# FROM DARKNESS TO LIGHT

*"I will rescue you from both your own people and the Gentiles.
Yes, I am sending you to the Gentiles to open their eyes, so they
may turn from darkness to light and from the power of Satan to
God. Then they will receive forgiveness for their sins and be given
a place among God's people, who are set apart by faith in me."*

ACTS 26:17-18 NLT

When it comes to forgiveness, God doesn't fool around. For proof, look no further than the life of Paul.

Before his conversion, Paul was called Saul. He actively persecuted Christians, and he even watched as Stephen was stoned (Acts 7:54-58). But then Jesus grabbed his attention. . .by striking him blind. He told Saul his new purpose: to open the eyes of others so that they could turn from darkness to light. These new believers would then receive forgiveness for their sins and join the company of God's people, set apart from nonbelievers.

If Jesus was that radical about forgiveness, all believers should stand up and take notice. We must strive to open the world's eyes to the light and blessing that comes from the One who holds the universe in His hands.

*Lord, thank You for being radical, for rescuing me,
for showing me the way to Your light.*

## PRAYER JAR INSPIRATION:
*Keep me, Lord, in Your love and light!*

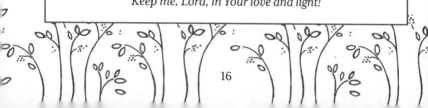

# THE EXTENT OF GOD'S FORGIVENESS

It's impossible to overstate the extent of God's forgiveness. When Jesus said from the cross, "It is finished" (John 19:30), He meant "paid in full." The death of God's Son satisfied sin's penalty for all sinners throughout history. Nothing else could've worked. This is why it's no longer necessary to offer the blood of animals as sacrifices for sin—it's already been taken care of.

It helps to see the sins in our life as God has seen them. Our view is confined to the present moment; the past is a memory, and the future is only a possibility. God, however, has no such limitations; He views our life in its totality.

God didn't save us only to regret it—He's always known everything we've done or will do. So when Jesus died for our sins, God had our entire life in view. He didn't give us eternal life only to take it back when we do something bad. The Lord already knew what sins we would commit as believers, but He forgave us anyway. However, the quality of our fellowship with God depends on constant confession of our sins as we become aware of them. First John 2:1 (KJV) says: "My little children, these things write I unto you, that ye sin not. And if any man sin, we have an advocate with the Father, Jesus Christ the righteous."

# SAFE AND SOUND

*God so greatly loved and dearly prized the world that He [even]*
*gave up His only begotten (unique) Son, so that whoever believes*
*in (trusts in, clings to, relies on) Him shall not perish (come to*
*destruction, be lost) but have eternal (everlasting) life. For God*
*did not send the Son into the world in order to judge (to reject,*
*to condemn, to pass sentence on) the world, but that the world*
*might find salvation and be made safe and sound through Him.*

JOHN 3:16-17 AMPC

God loves you to the moon and beyond! He loves you, His daughter,
so much that He gave up His only Son to save you. To cleanse you
from your sins. To set you free.

Your part in being saved is to simply believe in Jesus. To trust in
Him more than money, things, people, or other gods. You are to cling
to Him when your feet can find no purchase. You are to rely on Him
to meet all your needs.

When you believe, you're no longer subject to the penalty of sin;
instead, you gain eternal life with the God who loves you more than
anything in this world.

*Lord, in You I believe and trust. To You I cling. Thank You, God, for*
*sacrificing Your Son so that I, Your daughter, can live forever with You!*

## PRAYER JAR INSPIRATION:

*Through Jesus, I am safe and sound.*

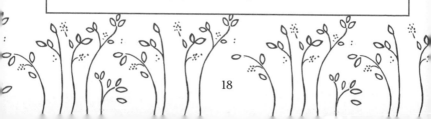

# FOR YOU

*When they came to a place called The Skull, they nailed
him to the cross. And the criminals were also crucified—one
on his right and one on his left. Jesus said, "Father, forgive
them, for they don't know what they are doing."*

Luke 23:33-34 nlt

Luke, the writer of the Gospel that bears his name, calmly lays out
all that happens to Jesus in His last days. . . .

For you, Jesus was put on trial. For you, an innocent Man was
judged, interrogated, and falsely accused. For you, God's Son quietly
bore insults, mocking, and degradation. For you, He was handed over
to the crowd, forced to walk to His place of execution, and nailed to
a cross, suspended between two criminals.

While hanging, Jesus prayed that God would forgive those who
had abused Him. For you, He died.

When you begin to wonder if God loves you, when you feel unforgivable and all alone in this world, remember what God allowed to
be sacrificed. He did it so that you would know that He loves you
and wants to embrace you—that He would rather lose His Son than
be separated from you.

God did it all for you.

*May I ever praise You, Lord, who sacrificed so much for me!*

## PRAYER JAR INSPIRATION:

*Your forgiveness for me is overwhelming!*

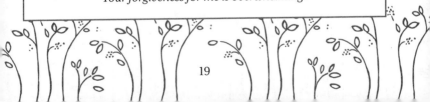

# OVERWHELMING PRAISE

*He has not dealt with us after our sins nor rewarded us according to our iniquities. For as the heavens are high above the earth, so great are His mercy and loving-kindness toward those who reverently and worshipfully fear Him.*

PSALM 103:10-11 AMPC

When we see people committing despicable acts, our outrage brings us to our feet in protest. We may even cry or shout out when witnessing their evil. And then, when those people receive their just desserts, we feel vindicated. Our hearts are less heavy, knowing the evildoers got what they deserve.

Yet, our God must have the same feelings of outrage when we hurt His heart by sinning. But even then, He is so merciful that He doesn't give us our just desserts. Instead, His mercy and love, His kindness and grace—which are higher than the heavens are above the earth—come flowing out toward us. Why? Because He is more benevolent toward us than we deserve.

Today, reflect on God's mercy and love. Consider that because He does not treat you as you deserve but instead forgives all that you do, He deserves more than just your obedience and love. He deserves immeasurable praise.

*Let me begin this day by lifting up a great amount of praise to You, Lord!*

## PRAYER JAR INSPIRATION:

*God's mercy and love overwhelm me!*

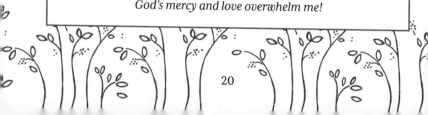

# ETERNAL LOVE

*You see, God takes all our crimes—our seemingly inexhaustible
sins—and removes them. As far as east is from the west, He removes
them from us. An earthly father expresses love for his children; it is
no different with our heavenly Father; the Eternal shows His love
for those who revere Him. For He knows what we are made of;
He knows our frame is frail, and He remembers we came from dust.*

Psalm 103:12-14 voice

God doesn't just forgive our countless misdeeds. He actually *removes*
them from us! The sins that once stained our souls vanish. They are
removed as far as the east is from the west.

That makes God the best Father in the universe. He is incomparable!
He is wonderful! He is heavenly! His love can never be measured!

If you're wondering why God is so good to those who worship
Him and respect His might and power, it's because He knows who
we are. He knows that we are but dust. That our frame is frail, that
our souls sometimes wander from His will. He knows that we sometimes have difficulty bearing up. And He cannot help but look upon
us with compassion.

*Thank You, Lord, for Your immense love and compassion.
May I follow Your example in my own life.*

## PRAYER JAR INSPIRATION:

*My God forgives and removes my sins with
His eternal love and compassion!*

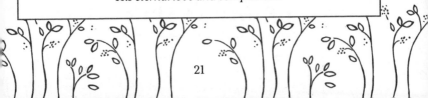

# GOD OF SECOND CHANCES: PART 1

*"I cried out to the Lord in my great trouble, and he answered me.
I called to you from the land of the dead, and Lord, you heard me!"*

Jonah 2:2 NLT

God called Jonah to go to the great city of Nineveh, where he was to pronounce that the wickedness of its people had caught the Lord's attention.

This bad news was not a message Jonah wanted to deliver. So, instead of going to Nineveh, he went to Joppa and boarded a ship going to Tarshish. But God wasn't done with him. He sent a violent storm to rock Jonah's boat.

Jonah, realizing God was sending him a not-so-subtle message, convinced the sailors to toss him into the sea. As soon as they did, "the storm stopped at once!" (Jonah 1:15 NLT). But God, still not done with His rebellious prophet, "arranged for a great fish to swallow Jonah" (Jonah 1:17 NLT). From inside the fish, Jonah cried out to God. In response, "the Lord ordered the fish to spit Jonah out onto the beach" (Jonah 2:10 NLT). God not only forgave the renegade prophet but gave him a second chance to do the right thing.

Today, consider how many second chances God has given you. And praise Him for doing so!

*Thank You, Lord, for both forgiving me and
giving me another chance to do right!*

---

## PRAYER JAR INSPIRATION:

*My forgiving God allows me second chances.*

# GOD OF SECOND CHANCES: PART 2

*God saw their works, that they turned from their evil way; and God revoked His [sentence of] evil that He had said that He would do to them and He did not do it [for He was comforted and eased concerning them].*

JONAH 3:10 AMPC

God is relentless in His willingness to forgive and offer second chances. Even after the prophet Jonah ran away to avoid warning Nineveh of God's judgment, God forgave and then recommissioned him.

Now realigned with God's direction, Jonah announced to the people, "Yet forty days and Nineveh shall be overthrown!" (Jonah 3:4 AMPC).

It was the faith of the people of Nineveh—their belief in God— that brought them to fast and mourn over Jonah's message. Even the king of Nineveh "covered himself with sackcloth, and sat in ashes" (Jonah 3:6 AMPC), hoping God would forgive and relent. And He did!

This doesn't mean we should continue to disobey God until He threatens us or chases us down. We *should* promptly change tack as soon as we realize the error of our ways. Yet, at the same time, it's good to know God will give us second chances when we prove to be more stubborn than we should.

*Help me, Lord, to make sure my ways are aligned with Yours!*

## PRAYER JAR INSPIRATION:

*Lord, thank You for Your unrelenting forgiveness!*

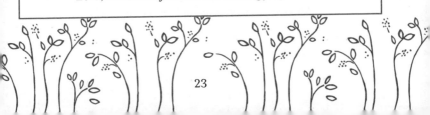

# GOD'S PROGRAM OF FORGIVENESS

*Jonah was furious. He lost his temper. He yelled at God, "God! I knew it—when I was back home, I knew this was going to happen! That's why I ran off to Tarshish! I knew you were sheer grace and mercy, not easily angered, rich in love, and ready at the drop of a hat to turn your plans of punishment into a program of forgiveness!"*

JONAH 4:1-2 MSG

Poor Jonah. Now that God had relented from destroying Nineveh, Jonah complained to Him about what He'd done! He had the gall to yell at His Creator and Sustainer, to gripe at the fact that He is so rich in love that He's always eager to turn His punishment into forgiveness!

God's response to Jonah's irrational tirade? "What do you have to be angry about?" (Jonah 4:4 MSG). But that didn't keep Jonah from stomping out of the city and sulking in the shade. That's when God caused a gourd to spring up and shelter Jonah to cool him off. But then God sent a worm that bored into the gourd and killed it. When Jonah prayed for death, God "mercifully reprove[d] him who would pity himself and this gourd, and yet would keep God from showing his compassion to so many thousand people" (Geneva Study Bible).

*Lord, thank You for Your amazing compassion no matter whom You bestow it upon!*

## PRAYER JAR INSPIRATION:
*My God has a program of forgiveness for all!*

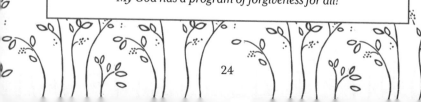

# THE SLATE WIPED CLEAN

*When you were stuck in your old sin-dead life, you were incapable*
*of responding to God. God brought you alive—right along with*
*Christ! Think of it! All sins forgiven, the slate wiped clean, that*
*old arrest warrant canceled and nailed to Christ's cross.*

COLOSSIANS 2:13-14 MSG

Because of Jesus, you've been transformed. Instead of being dead in
your sins and alienated from God, you are a new woman with a new
life! Every sin and mistake you've ever committed has been forgiven.
All those black marks against you have been erased from you and
added to Christ's cross. You've been reborn!

That's one major do-over! The question now is: Where will you
go from here? In what ways are you going to thank God for this
miraculous erasure? How are you going to repay a debt that could
never be repaid?

As you live your new life with a clean slate, one thing you can do is
to show as much mercy and love to others as God has shown to you.

*Help me, Lord, find a way to show love and mercy to everyone I meet!*

---

## PRAYER JAR INSPIRATION:

*Because of Jesus' love and God's mercy, I am alive*
*and forgiven! I am a woman reborn!*

# SET FREE IN FORGIVENESS

*Visualize this: His blood freely flowing down the cross, setting us free! We are forgiven for our sinful ways by the richness of His grace, which He has poured all over us. With all wisdom and insight, He has enlightened us to the great mystery at the center of His will. With immense pleasure, He laid out His intentions through Jesus, a plan that will climax when the time is right as He returns to create order and unity—both in heaven and on earth—when all things are brought together under the Anointed's royal rule.*

<small>EPHESIANS 1:7-10 VOICE</small>

Close your eyes. Imagine your body, spirit, soul, and mind being immersed in God's grace and soaked in His forgiveness. Streams of mercy flow freely within and without. God has poured His grace all over you. What an amazing picture!

Think of how precious you are to God. He has bequeathed wisdom and insight to you. You're now clued into His plan and the mystery of His will.

Because you are one with the Word (Jesus), you can rest assured not only that you are forgiven but that He will one day return and make *all* things right!

*You amaze me, Lord! Thank You for making me a part of Your grand plan!*

## PRAYER JAR INSPIRATION:

*Forgiveness and grace flow freely from my God!*

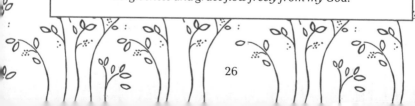

# FORGIVEN AND FORGOTTEN

*So let's get this clear: it's for My own sake that I save
you. I am He who wipes the slate clean and erases your
wrongdoing. I will not call to mind your sins anymore.*

ISAIAH 43:25 VOICE

How great is your God? He is so great, loving, wonderful, and full of mercy that He wipes the slate clean of your sin. Whatever charges are against you—whatever ways you've erred, disobeyed, or taken the wrong path—He pardons. Then, He goes a step further by never again even thinking about the errors you've made!

Why? Why would a holy God forgive and forget your wrongs?

It's not because *you* can pardon sin. No, that's His role alone. And neither is it because you have any power to coerce Him into doing so. Instead, the reason God forgives and forgets is because He wants to show the world how much love and compassion He feels toward you—how *He alone* can wipe away your wrongs.

Today, meditate on the fact that God has made you innocent. Realize that He alone can wipe your slate clean. Then praise Him for the love and compassion that prompts Him to fully forgive and forget.

*I praise Your name, Lord, for Your love and
compassion that erase my record of wrongs!*

## PRAYER JAR INSPIRATION:

*My God both forgives and forgets!*

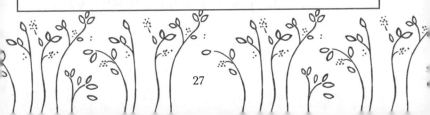

# ONE SACRIFICE FOR ALL

*"This is the new covenant I will make with my people on that day, says the LORD: I will put my laws in their hearts, and I will write them on their minds." Then he says, "I will never again remember their sins and lawless deeds." And when sins have been forgiven, there is no need to offer any more sacrifices.*

HEBREWS 10:16-18 NLT

Under the old agreement with God, a priest had to make daily sacrifices so that the people would be cleansed of sin. But this method never solved the sin problem. Then, Jesus came along. He sacrificed His own body once and for all, and *voila!* This single sacrifice took away sins for all time. Jesus Christ's death "was a perfect sacrifice by a perfect person to perfect some very imperfect people" (Hebrews 10:14 MSG). His work alone "completely cleansed and perfected those who are consecrated and made holy" (Hebrews 10:14 AMPC).

The Holy Spirit backed this up by prompting the prophet Jeremiah to pronounce this new covenant, one that would not be written on stones (as the Ten Commandments were) but on peoples' hearts and minds (Jeremiah 31:33). Now, God forgives and forgets His peoples' wrongdoing—no additional sacrifice required.

Oh, what a God! Oh, what a Savior!

*Spirit of God, thank You for reminding us that Jesus Christ's work has—in one fell swoop—saved and sanctified all, including me!*

## PRAYER JAR INSPIRATION:

*Thank You, Jesus, for Your single great sacrifice for me!*

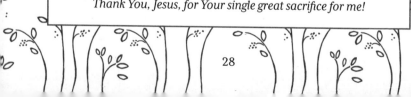

# GOOD AND CLEAN

*Learn to do good; commit yourselves to seeking justice. Make right for the world's most vulnerable—the oppressed, the orphaned, the widow. Come on now, let's walk and talk; let's work this out. Your wrongdoings are bloodred, but they can turn as white as snow. Your sins are red like crimson, but they can be made clean again like new wool.*

ISAIAH 1:17-18 VOICE

God continually tries to get His people to stop doing evil. He wants them to turn to good, to seek justice, to make things right for the afflicted, homeless, parentless, and widowed. Why? Because God wants His people to be like Him. To show mercy, love, and compassion. To remember that He made us for good and that good things come to those who do good!

There's no stain tougher to remove than blood. But God is the doer of the impossible. There's no challenge He can't meet, no problem He can't solve, no sin He can't cleanse, no wrong He can't right.

So, while Jesus has saved you once and for all from your sins, the Word still urges you to be like Him: good, loving, forgiving, and merciful, seeking justice for all.

Look around your corner of the world. How can you lift someone who's down today?

*Lord, please show me where and how I can bring more good into this world!*

## PRAYER JAR INSPIRATION:

*With God's help, I am good and clean!*

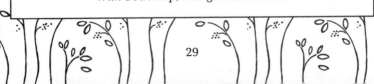

29

# AFTER GOD'S OWN HEART: PART 1

*David sent messengers to get her, and when she came to him,
he slept with her. Now she had just been purifying herself from
her uncleanness. Afterward, she returned home. The woman
conceived and sent word to inform David: "I am pregnant."*

2 SAMUEL 11:4-5 HCSB

One spring, King David had been hanging at home in Jerusalem while his soldiers were out fighting. Perhaps a bit bored, he strolled out onto his roof and happened to see Bathsheba, a married woman, bathing. Unable to resist temptation, David had her brought to him. After they slept together, Bathsheba sent word to David that she was pregnant. There was no question the child was his.

Over the next several days, David attempted to cover up his misdeed by having Uriah, Bathsheba's husband, sent to the front battle lines where he was eventually killed. Then, when Bathsheba's days of mourning were over, David took her to be his wife.

Thus, David committed both adultery and murder, which was seen as "evil in the sight of the Lord" (2 Samuel 11:27 AMPC). So, God prompted Nathan the prophet to help David understand what he'd done.

When we do wrong, there's no hiding it from God. God's light has a way of illuminating our darkness (2 Samuel 12:12).

*Forgive me, Lord, for ever thinking I could hide any misdeeds from You.*

## PRAYER JAR INSPIRATION:

*My God sees—and knows—all.*

# AFTER GOD'S OWN HEART: PART 2

*David confessed to Nathan, "I have sinned against the LORD." Nathan replied, "Yes, but the LORD has forgiven you, and you won't die for this sin. Nevertheless, because you have shown utter contempt for the word of the LORD by doing this, your child will die."*

2 SAMUEL 12:13–14 NLT

David did sin—big time! Not only did he sleep with a married woman, but he had her husband put into the thick of battle where he was killed. David could not hide his misdeeds—adultery, lying, and murder—from the God who sees all.

And although God did forgive David's actions, he still had to suffer the consequences. In this instance, the baby that resulted from David's sin became ill and died.

Yet, even with all these sins laid at David's door, he was still a man after God's own heart (Acts 13:22), the proverbial apple of God's eye (Psalm 17:8). Why? Because David had absolute faith in God. When he sinned, he not only admitted it but was sincerely remorseful.

Although you too may sometimes lose your way, strive to be a person after God's own heart, demonstrating the strength of your faith and dedication to God and admitting when you fall short.

*Show me, Lord, how to be a woman after Your heart!*

## PRAYER JAR INSPIRATION:
*Increase my faith, Lord! May I become the apple of Your eye!*

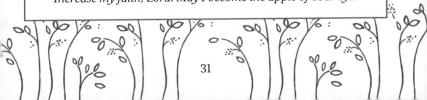

# THE LOVE OF GOD

*Love is patient; love is kind. Love isn't envious, doesn't boast,*
*brag, or strut about. There's no arrogance in love; it's never rude,*
*crude, or indecent—it's not self-absorbed. Love isn't easily upset.*
*Love doesn't tally wrongs or celebrate injustice; but truth—yes,*
*truth—is love's delight! Love puts up with anything and everything*
*that comes along; it trusts, hopes, and endures no matter what.*

1 Corinthians 13:4-7 voice

First John 4:16 (voice) teaches that "God is love. Anyone who lives faithfully in love also lives faithfully in God, and God lives in him." And since God is love, it only stands to reason that God is also all the things listed in 1 Corinthians 13! Love (a.k.a. God) is patient and kind. It is not self-absorbed but selfless. Nor is it easily angered. It doesn't keep a record of wrongs, and it delights in truth!

First Corinthians 13 is a wonder-filled description of who God is. Hearing that love puts up with everything rings true, especially when we remember all our past missteps. . .and all the times God has forgiven and forgotten those misdeeds.

Today, reflect on how much God loves you. Then, think of some ways you can reflect His love to others.

*Lord, I am overwhelmed with gratitude for*
*Your extravagant love for me!*

## PRAYER JAR INSPIRATION:

*May I live as a reflection of God's love!*

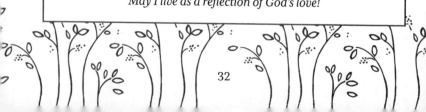

# LAVISH WITH FORGIVENESS

*Seek God while he's here to be found, pray to him while he's close at hand. Let the wicked abandon their way of life and the evil their way of thinking. Let them come back to God, who is merciful, come back to our God, who is lavish with forgiveness.*

ISAIAH 55:6-7 MSG

Every morning, God's Word reaches out to you, wanting to bring you closer to Him. While He is near, pray to Him. Spend time in His presence. Ask Him to tell you what He wants you to do, say, be, and desire. . .and what He wants you to give up or turn over to Him.

To get your head on straight—your heart and will aligned with God's—ask Him to change your thinking, to fill your mind with love, kindness, humility, gentleness, and generosity. Ask Him to make you more like Him, transforming you into the woman He originally designed you to be. Run into His arms, confessing whatever is burdening your heart, whatever the Spirit is prompting you to put right. All the while, remember your God is lavish with forgiveness.

*Sensing Your nearness in this moment, Lord of my life, I come to You with all my thoughts, dreams, and actions. Change within me whatever is not of You. Bless me with Your lavish forgiveness.*

## PRAYER JAR INSPIRATION:

*I need not fear fessing up to my God, for He is lavish with forgiveness.*

# RESCUED FROM DARKNESS

*Thank You, Father, as You have made us eligible to receive our portion of the inheritance given to all those set apart by the light. You have rescued us from dark powers and brought us safely into the kingdom of Your Son, whom You love and in whom we are redeemed and forgiven of our sins [through His blood].*

COLOSSIANS 1:12-14 VOICE

What a wonderful thank-you prayer the apostle Paul sent to the church in Colossae. He made a point of telling his readers what God has done for those who believe in Him—a point we should take to heart today.

If you're looking to be rescued by a white knight, it's already happened! Because Jesus—God's one and only Son—took our sins upon Him, we've been saved, redeemed, and forgiven! We've been freed from the darkness and delivered into the light of Jesus' kingdom.

Know that no matter what happens in your life, you are no longer in the clutches of evil but in the arms of a Savior who loves you more than you can imagine!

*Lord of light, thank You for pursuing me, for rescuing me from the darkness so that I can live in the light of Your forgiveness and love!*

## PRAYER JAR INSPIRATION:

*God is my true knight in shining armor who has brought me into the light of forgiveness!*

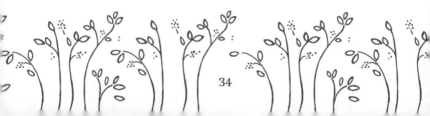

# MERCY IS GOD'S SPECIALTY

*Where is the god who can compare with you—wiping the slate clean of guilt, turning a blind eye, a deaf ear, to the past sins of your purged and precious people? You don't nurse your anger and don't stay angry long, for mercy is your specialty. That's what you love most. And compassion is on its way to us. You'll stamp out our wrongdoing. You'll sink our sins to the bottom of the ocean.*

MICAH 7:18-19 MSG

When it comes to mercy, love, and forgiveness, your God is incomparable. You can't gain such things from idols, possessions, or power. Only God can pardon all of your wrongdoing. Only He can purge you of sin's stain. But that's not all!

Your God will not hold a grudge against you. He won't give you the silent treatment nor abuse you for your past missteps. Instead, He'll shower you with His love, affection, and devotion. He'll look upon you with mercy and compassion. He'll correct the wrongs you've committed—and cast them all to the bottom of the ocean! So, whenever guilt and the fear of God's anger begins creeping into your heart, remember that mercy is His specialty.

*There is no one like You, Lord! Thank You for Your mercy!*

---

# PRAYER JAR INSPIRATION:

*God absolves me with His abundant mercy and compassion!*

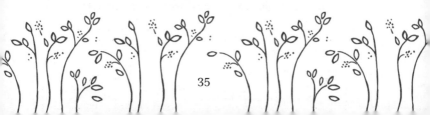

# AN IMPORTANT CAVEAT

*If you forgive people their trespasses [their reckless and willful
sins, leaving them, letting them go, and giving up resentment],
your heavenly Father will also forgive you. But if you do not
forgive others their trespasses [their reckless and willful sins,
leaving them, letting them go, and giving up resentment],
neither will your Father forgive you your trespasses.*

MATTHEW 6:14-15 AMPC

God is abundantly forgiving. But there is one caveat: to be forgiven
by Father God, you must forgive those who have sinned against you.

This caveat is so important that Jesus included it in the Lord's
Prayer! In Luke 11:4 (AMPC), the line reads: "And forgive us our sins,
for we ourselves also forgive everyone who is indebted to us [who has
offended us or done us wrong]." Matthew 6:12 (AMPC) puts it like
this: "And forgive us our debts, as we also have forgiven (left, remitted,
and let go of the debts, and have given up resentment against) our
debtors." But both mean the same thing: if you want God to lovingly
forgive you when you wrong Him, you must do the same to whoever
wrongs you.

Are you ready?

*Lord, help me find the compassion to forgive
others as You have forgiven me.*

## PRAYER JAR INSPIRATION:

*My God forgives me to the extent I forgive others!*

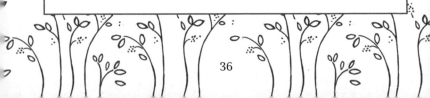

# RICH IN MERCY

*God, who is rich in mercy, because of His great love that He
had for us, made us alive with the Messiah even though we
were dead in trespasses. You are saved by grace! Together with
Christ Jesus He also raised us up and seated us in the heavens,
so that in the coming ages He might display the immeasurable
riches of His grace through His kindness to us in Christ Jesus.*

Ephesians 2:4-7 hcsb

Time after time, the Word tells us how rich God is in His mercy, how
immeasurable His kindness is to us fallible female followers. And it's
all due to His unfathomable and never-ending love for us!

When you begin to doubt the extent of God's forgiveness for you,
read today's verses. Remember that you are not just forgiven but made
alive with Christ! That God's grace has saved you from the darkness
and brought you into the light! That you have been raised up and
seated in the heavens with Jesus.

What blessings upon blessings!

*When I doubt the extent of Your forgiveness to me,
Lord, lead me to Your Word so that I can comprehend
the blessings upon blessings You shower on me!*

## PRAYER JAR INSPIRATION:

*All praise to God who is rich in mercy and has saved me by His grace!*

# SEEKING FORGIVENESS

We are forgiven by others when they let go of resentment and give up any demand for compensation. The Bible teaches that unselfish love is the basis for true forgiveness.

There is a process for seeking forgiveness. Talking about wanting to be forgiven is one thing, but facing the reality of the hurts we've caused an individual—and fully connecting with the emotions, damage, and consequences—is entirely different. Most of us deal inappropriately with the way we've hurt others. We don't understand the depth of the hurt we've caused, so we assume it will go away in time. But when we seek forgiveness, it's vital to remember and work through each event that occurred. If left unchecked, it will remain toxic—both to our own lives and to our relationships. It's important to evaluate our violations, praying about which ones must be addressed. God must be the one who directs the process, so it needs to be covered in prayer.

It may help to write down the names of those we have hurt and then place the paper in our prayer jar. Praying for people we've offended—as we're also in the process of seeking their forgiveness—will bring a sense of inner peace.

# HE WILL FORGIVE

*If My people, who are called by My name, shall humble*
*themselves, pray, seek, crave, and require of necessity*
*My face and turn from their wicked ways, then will I hear*
*from heaven, forgive their sin, and heal their land.*

2 Chronicles 7:14 ampc

Having built a temple for God's presence, King Solomon then prayed to the Lord (2 Chronicles 6). He began by praising His name, proclaiming that He was like no other God in the heavens or earth. Why? Because this God keeps His promises and shows love and mercy to those who walk before Him with all their hearts. King Solomon then asked God to hear the prayers of His people and forgive them.

After Solomon's prayer, the Lord's glory filled the entire temple. Later that night, He appeared to Solomon, telling him that if His people humble themselves, pray, seek after and crave His face, and "abandon any actions or thoughts that might lead to further sinning" (2 Chronicles 7:14 voice), then God would forgive them.

To this day, God keeps His promises. If you follow the prayer outline in today's verses, He will hear. . .and He will forgive.

*I humble myself before You, Lord. Hear my prayer.*

## PRAYER JAR INSPIRATION:

*God hears—me! God heals—me! God forgives—me!*

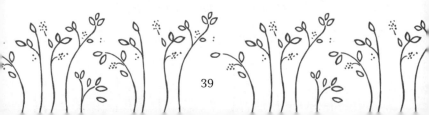

# MAKING THINGS RIGHT

*Eternal One (to Moses): Tell the Israelites that sinning against each other is just like abandoning Me.*

NUMBERS 5:6 VOICE

God clearly teaches that when His people commit a wrong against someone else, they are abandoning all God stands for. In other words, the perpetrators are actually committing a wrong against God Himself!

In Leviticus 19:18 (VOICE), God told His followers to "love your neighbor as you love yourself." Why? "For I am the Eternal One." In other words, God is saying, "Do this because I told you so. I'm in charge!" Thus, when you do someone wrong, a big part of your confession and apology must go not only to the party you've injured but to the Big Guy Himself! And there's no expiration date to this edict. No matter how long it's been, God and whomever you've injured need to hear your apology. And God wants you to make things right in whatever way you can.

Today, think about someone who needs an apology from you. Consider how you might try to make things right. Then, start by seeking God and confessing it to Him in prayer. If needed, ask Him to help you confess to the one you've harmed. . .and find a way to make things right.

*I confess, Lord, that I have done wrong. Hear my prayer.*

## PRAYER JAR INSPIRATION:

*God, help me make things right.*

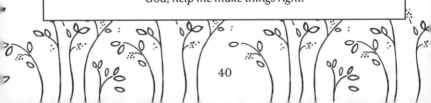

# NO FOOLING

*If we claim that we're free of sin, we're only fooling ourselves. A claim like that is errant nonsense. On the other hand, if we admit our sins—simply come clean about them—he won't let us down; he'll be true to himself. He'll forgive our sins and purge us of all wrongdoing. If we claim that we've never sinned, we out-and-out contradict God—make a liar out of him. A claim like that only shows off our ignorance of God.*

1 JOHN 1:8-10 MSG

None of us are perfect. At some point, we're going to trip, stumble, or downright fall from the path God has outlined for us in His Word. The apostle John makes it clear in today's passage that if we don't admit this, we're only fooling ourselves.

On the other hand, if we admit that we have done wrong and confess our mistakes to God, He will do what He does best: He'll forgive us and rinse us off! And He'll do so over and over again for as many times as it takes to get us back on the right track.

*Thank You, Lord, for reminding me that no one*
*is perfect. . .but that You will forgive all!*

## PRAYER JAR INSPIRATION:

*Praise the God who forgives faulty females!*

41

# HIDING SIN AWAY: PART 1

*The Lord said to Joshua, . . . "Israel has sinned and broken my covenant! They have stolen some of the things that I commanded must be set apart for me. And they have not only stolen them but have lied about it and hidden the things among their own belongings."*

JOSHUA 7:10-11 NLT

Proverbs 28:13 (VOICE) tells us: "Whoever tries to hide his sins will not succeed, but the one who confesses his sins and leaves them behind will find mercy." This truth is borne out in a story that goes back to the days of Joshua.

God had made it clear that everything the Israelites gleaned when conquering and plundering Jericho had to be destroyed. But a man named Achan took some things and hid them away.

After Jericho fell, Joshua sent some soldiers to invade the city of Ai. . .and was met with a quick defeat. Upon hearing of this failure, the Israelites' courage "melted away like water" (Joshua 7:5 VOICE). So Joshua asked God where they'd gone wrong. That's when God revealed that someone had sinned and, instead of confessing, had hidden his misdeed.

Remember, God sees all. Are you trying to hide anything?

*Lord, search me to see if there is a hidden sin I need to drag out into the light. Bring it to my mind, help me confess it, and then please forgive me.*

## PRAYER JAR INSPIRATION:

*God, help me admit all to You all the time.*

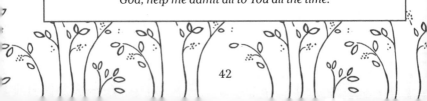

# HIDING SIN AWAY: PART 2

*Why have you brought trouble on us? The Lord will trouble you this day.*

JOSHUA 7:25 AMPC

God had told the Israelites not to keep any plunder from Jericho because its residents followed pagan gods. The Lord didn't want His people cherishing and then worshipping false idols. So when the Israelites were soundly defeated at Ai and Joshua asked God why, the Lord told him it was because someone had not only disobeyed God but then tried to cover it up! All this made God extremely angry.

With God's help, Joshua discovered who the culprit was, and Achan confessed he had broken God's commandment: "Among the spoils of the city, I found a beautiful Babylonian robe, 5 pounds of silver, and 20 ounces of gold. When I saw them, I wanted them and I took them. They are buried now in the ground inside my tent" (Joshua 7:21 VOICE).

Our eyes can lead us into the worst misdeeds. Just as Eve saw and took the fruit, Achan saw and took these riches. If he'd seen things with the eyes of faith, he could've spared himself, his family, and Israel a *lot* of trouble.

*Lord, help me see with the eyes of faith, keeping my focus on You instead of things. But if I do trip up, may I quickly come to You and confess all!*

## PRAYER JAR INSPIRATION:

*May I covet nothing but You, my Lord.*

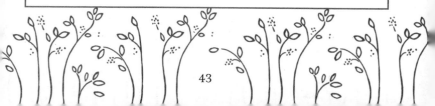

43

# HOLY TRUTHS

*Ananias, have you allowed Satan to influence your lies to the*
*Holy Spirit and hold back some of the money? Look, it was*
*your property before you sold it, and the money was all yours*
*after you sold it. Why have you concocted this scheme in your*
*heart? You weren't just lying to us; you were lying to God.*

ACTS 5:3-4 VOICE

The community of Christian believers in Jerusalem were deeply united in heart and soul, sharing their possessions with each other. Many even sold their land and houses and brought the money to the church leaders to distribute among all! As a result, no one lived in need.

Then one day, a man named Ananias and his wife Sapphira sold some property but kept back some of the proceeds. Yet Ananias "pretended to make a full donation to the Lord's emissaries" (Acts 5:2 VOICE). He could've been honest and said it was a partial donation. But instead, Ananias decided to deceive. In doing so, he was lying not only to his fellow believers but to God. The result: Ananias was struck dead where he stood!

Even a half-truth can trip you up. To live a full life (instead of a *fool's* life), you must be totally honest with yourself and with God.

*Help me, Lord, to be a woman of holy truths—not half-truths!*

## PRAYER JAR INSPIRATION:

*May I be a woman of truth, belonging to the God of truth!*

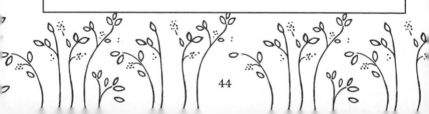

# HEARTFELT REMORSE

*David arose [in the darkness] and stealthily cut off the skirt of*
*Saul's robe. Afterward, David's heart smote him because he*
*had cut off Saul's skirt. He said to his men, The Lord forbid that*
*I should do this to my master, the Lord's anointed, to put my*
*hand out against him, when he is the anointed of the Lord.*

1 SAMUEL 24:4-6 AMPC

When the prophet Samuel anointed David, "the Spirit of the LORD came powerfully upon David from that day on" (1 Samuel 16:13 NLT).

Sometime later, while King Saul was hunting David, the former went into a cave to relieve himself. Little did he know, David and his men were hiding in the recesses of that same cave.

Encouraged by the baser instincts of his men, David crept quietly toward Saul and secretly cut off a part of his robe. But as soon as David had done the deed, his conscience and the Holy Spirit worked in tandem to let him know he'd done wrong.

David's heart led him to confess to Saul. His speech to the king brought Saul to tears, prompting him to say, "May the Eternal reward you richly for the good you have done for me today" (1 Samuel 24:19 VOICE).

May you, like David, follow the promptings of your conscience and the Holy Spirit, expressing your heartfelt remorse to those who need to hear it.

*Lead me, Spirit, to confess when You prompt me.*

## PRAYER JAR INSPIRATION:

*The Lord holds my tender heart in His hand.*

# WORD WATCHERS

*For the mouth simply shapes the heart's impulses into words.*
*And so the good man (who is filled with goodness) speaks good*
*words, while the evil man (who is filled with evil) speaks evil*
*words. I tell you this: on the day of judgment, people will be*
*called to account for every careless word they have ever said.*
MATTHEW 12:34-36 VOICE

Your mouth can get you into a whole lot of trouble—not just in this life but in the one to come! On Judgment Day, "the righteous will be acquitted by their own words, and. . .evildoers will be condemned by [their] own words" (Matthew 12:37 VOICE).

Jesus makes it clear that what comes out of your mouth can come back to haunt you. Like actions, words can never be taken back. Once they've left your mouth, they stay out there, ricocheting and perhaps finding homes in your hearers' minds.

The point? Watch your words. Don't let your tongue form anything that can wound. Keep your head and heart in God's Word and your mouth on alert. Become a good woman who, filled with goodness, speaks only good words!

*Help me, Lord, to keep my mind and heart on*
*You. . .and a careful eye on my mouth!*

## PRAYER JAR INSPIRATION:
*Fill my heart with good, Lord, so that my words please You!*

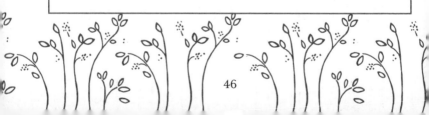

46

# FAULTS AND FORGIVENESS

*Your servant will find, hidden in Your commandments, both
a strong warning and a great reward for keeping them. Who
could possibly know all that he has done wrong? Forgive my
hidden and unknown faults. As I am Your servant, protect me
from my bent toward pride, and keep sin from ruling my life.*

PSALM 19:11-13 VOICE

Let's face it: we all have our faults. We are fallible females. That's not
an excuse—just a fact.

Because not one of us is perfect, we sometimes err and don't realize
it. So while our life aim is to keep God's commands so that we can find
our way in the darkness, we still want to go deeper. We want God to
shine His light within us and cleanse us from our unconscious faults.

The fact that God has the power to bring these hidden faults to
light and forgive them is an absolute blessing. For He can save us
from any pride and sin that may be working their way to the surface.
Ask God today to take those faults away.

*Lord, You know me inside and out. Please forgive my hidden faults!*

## PRAYER JAR INSPIRATION:

*Shine Your light within me, Lord! Forgive what lies hidden.*

# THE HOLY HELPER

*Here's my instruction: walk in the Spirit, and let the Spirit bring order to your life. If you do, you will never give in to your selfish and sinful cravings. For everything the flesh desires goes against the Spirit, and everything the Spirit desires goes against the flesh. There is a constant battle raging between them that prevents you from doing the good you want to do. But when you are led by the Spirit, you are no longer subject to the law.*

GALATIANS 5:16-18 VOICE

God continues to hold the power of forgiveness in His hands. And He wants us to run to Him at the first sign of a misstep, to tell Him all and ask His forgiveness. However, He also gives us a Helper, One who can keep us from stumbling in the first place. That holy Helper is the Spirit.

To keep you from wandering off God's way and stepping into sin, the apostle Paul provides instructions: walk in the Spirit and allow Him to rule over your life. When you let the Spirit overrule the flesh, all your selfish and sinful cravings will dissipate!

*Teach me, Lord, how to walk in the Spirit!*

---

## PRAYER JAR INSPIRATION:

*Thank You, Lord, for Your gift of the Spirit!*

# SPIRIT WALKER

*Walk and live [habitually] in the [Holy] Spirit [responsive to and controlled and guided by the Spirit]; then you will certainly not gratify the cravings and desires of the flesh (of human nature without God).*

GALATIANS 5:16 AMPC

It's great that we have access to the Holy Spirit, One who is ready, willing, and able to help us stick to God's way and not veer off in a sinful direction. But how do we walk in the Spirit?

To get yourself on the Spirit's wavelength, you must pray—and commit to doing so all day, every day. You also need to trust that God knows best. That means when the Spirit prompts you, you should follow His lead, regardless of whatever else seems the "better" path.

To build up your prayer muscle and your trust in God, tell Him at the end of every day what you're grateful for. And mean it! Consider writing down your blessings. This will make an impression upon your heart, spirit, and mind. And it's easy enough to remember once you start doing it.

Last, but certainly not least, keep your eyes and thoughts on Jesus. Make His Word the first thing you read in the morning and the last thing you read at night!

*Lord, make me a Spirit walker, following His lead, not mine!*

---

## PRAYER JAR INSPIRATION:
*Lead me, Lord, down the Spirit-led pathway to You!*

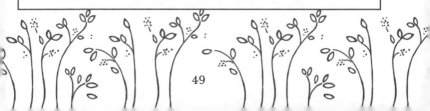

# HUMBLE PRAYERS

*He also told this parable to some people who trusted in themselves and were confident that they were righteous [that they were upright and in right standing with God] and scorned and made nothing of all the rest of men.*

LUKE 18:9 AMPC

Some people are so pleased with themselves that they don't think they need forgiveness. After all, when you're perfect—when you're always doing and saying the "right" things—there's no need for God to forgive you. Right?

Jesus addressed this issue with a parable about two men—one a Pharisee, the other a tax collector—who went to the temple to pray.

The Pharisee stood up and declared, "I thank you, God, that I am not like other people—cheaters, sinners, adulterers. I'm certainly not like that tax collector! I fast twice a week, and I give you a tenth of my income" (Luke 18:11-12 NLT). The tax collector, however, "stood at a distance and dared not even lift his eyes to heaven. . . . Instead, he beat his chest in sorrow, saying, 'O God, be merciful to me, for I am a sinner'" (Luke 18:13 NLT).

Jesus made His point, saying, "This sinner, not the Pharisee, returned home justified before God. For those who exalt themselves will be humbled, and those who humble themselves will be exalted" (Luke 18:14 NLT).

Which of "those" are you?

*Merciful God, I come asking Your forgiveness.*

## PRAYER JAR INSPIRATION:

*May I pray each day with a humble heart!*

# WOMAN BLESSED FOUR WAYS

*Blessed (happy, fortunate, to be envied) is he who has forgiveness
of his transgression continually exercised upon him, whose sin is
covered. Blessed (happy, fortunate, to be envied) is the man to whom
the Lord imputes no iniquity and in whose spirit there is no deceit.*
PSALM 32:1-2 AMPC

When you're counting your blessings at night, thanking God for all He does, don't forget to mention how happy you are for His continual forgiveness. Each time you confess your missteps, God is there to listen and to grant you His forgiveness (blessing number 1). He then wipes your slate clean, removing your sins far out of sight (blessing number 2).

God's next blessing (number 3) is that He doesn't bear a grudge! Once you've been forgiven, He holds nothing against you—so neither should you! And finally, blessing number 4 stems from how clean and honest your spirit becomes when you are upfront with God about your wrongdoings. Whew! Doesn't that feel great?

Examine yourself today. If you've been hiding something from God, run into His arms. Tell Him all, holding nothing back. Those four blessings await!

*Lord, help me examine myself and bring all my missteps before You.*

---

## PRAYER JAR INSPIRATION:

*God's forgiveness is a four-fold blessing! What joy!*

---

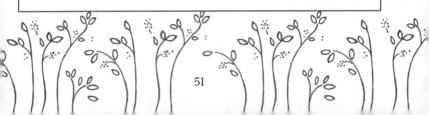

# IN PRAISE OF PROMISES
# CONTINUALLY KEPT

*O Eternal One, Israel's God, there is no other God who compares to You
in heaven or on earth. You have guarded Your covenant and revealed
Your loyal love to those who serve You with all their being. You have kept
Your word to Your servant, my father, David. You have promised with
Your mouth and fulfilled Your promise with Your actions as it is today.*

1 Kings 8:23-24 voice

When King Solomon finished building the Lord's temple, he prayed
a prayer of dedication which covered a myriad of topics. . .and which
gives us an excellent example of how we, too, should pray.

The first thing Solomon did in his prayer was to praise God,
declaring that there is no God that compares to Him. For this, God
not only keeps His agreements intact but proves His loyalty by lovingly
providing for those who follow Him with all their hearts. Each day,
we experience the fulfillment of His promises.

Before praying to God for forgiveness, spend some time in praise.
Think back to the promises He has kept. Know that He will continue
to pardon and provide.

*You are a God like no other, Lord. . . .*

## PRAYER JAR INSPIRATION:
*My God keeps His promises!*

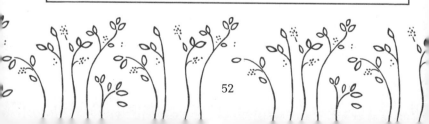

# THE BEST PATH

*When the heavens are dried up and no rain is given to the earth*
*because Your people sinned against You, if they turn and pray in*
*the direction of this place and praise Your name and turn away*
*from their sins after You afflict them, then hear them in heaven and*
*forgive the sins of those who serve You and of Your people Israel.*
*Show them the best path, the good path, upon which to walk.*

1 KINGS 8:35-36 VOICE

Sometimes, God teaches us by our troubles. This portion of Solomon's prayer reminds us that everything we receive is a blessing from God. And when something is held back from us, it's time to take stock of where we've been, where we are, and where we're headed.

With each misstep, consider where, how, and *why* you stumbled. Your thoughts may be so scattered that you need God to tell you where you went wrong. Then you need to ask God to not only forgive you but show you a better way.

*Lord, where did I go wrong? Lead me down a better path.*

## PRAYER JAR INSPIRATION:
*My God forgives and then guides me to the best path, the good path.*

# HEARTFELT PRAYERS

*Hear in heaven, Your dwelling place, and forgive and act and give to every man according to his ways, whose heart You know, for You and You only know the hearts of all the children of men, that they may fear and revere You all the days that they live in the land.*

1 KINGS 8:39-40 AMPC

When you come to God and confess your missteps, He knows if you're being sincere. He knows if you are truly sorry for what you've said or done. For God alone knows your heart. He knows what's within it and what comes out of it.

So when you open yourself up to God, you must be honest. After praising Him, perhaps you could ask God to search your heart and to point out any wrong intentions that may lurk therein. Ask Him to correct any fault He finds. Perhaps you're misjudging someone. Perhaps you're going down the wrong path. Perhaps what your heart intends is not what God intends for you.

The point is to remember to whom you're talking: Someone who knows you better than you know yourself. So, go to Him with your heart on your sleeve, questions on your lips, praises and petitions on your tongue. Let your prayer be heartfelt.

*Lord, You know me better than I do myself. Make me "heart smart."*

## PRAYER JAR INSPIRATION:
*God knows my heart best.*

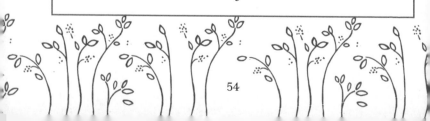

# TESTING, ONE AND TWO

*"You're talking like an empty-headed fool. We take the good days from God—why not also the bad days?" Not once through all this did Job sin. He said nothing against God.*

JOB 2:10 MSG

Job was a blameless and upright man who lost everything when God allowed Satan to test him. In his first test, God told Satan he could do what he wanted with Job except cause him bodily injury. Consequently, Job lost his servants, livestock, and children. He responded to the situation by saying, "I came naked from my mother's womb, and I will be naked when I leave. The LORD gave me what I had, and the LORD has taken it away. Praise the name of the LORD!" (Job 1:21 NLT). "In all of this, Job did not sin by blaming God" (Job 1:22 NLT).

For the second test, God allowed Satan to harm Job physically but not kill him. Soon, Job's body was covered with boils. He sat in an ash heap, scraping his sores with broken pottery. When his wife told him to curse God and die, Job said, "Should we accept only good things from the hand of God and never anything bad?" (Job 2:10 NLT). "Throughout all of this, Job did not sin with his mouth; he would not curse God as the Accuser predicted" (Job 2:10 VOICE).

*Lord, may Your name forever remain unsullied in my heart and mind!*

## PRAYER JAR INSPIRATION:

*May my lips always praise the Lord!*

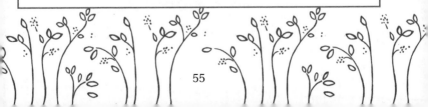

# SKEWED PRAYERS: PART 1

*"What are mortals anyway, that you bother with them, that you even give them the time of day? That you check up on them every morning, looking in on them to see how they're doing? Let up on me, will you? Can't you even let me spit in peace?"*

JOB 7:17-19 MSG

Pain and tears test Job's resolve. He begins to lose hope, and his prayers become skewed.

Instead of seeing God as a watchful shepherd, Job asks why He continually spies upon mortals as if He were just waiting to see them slip up so that He can punish them. Job goes so far as to ask God to just let up on him already! He cannot take any more of this pain and heartbreak.

Perhaps you, too, have at times asked God why He never seems to give you a break. But that's skewed thinking *and* praying. God cares for you. He's looking to forgive and love, not to take gleeful revenge. In response to Job's prayer, we can say with the psalmist, "What are mere mortals that you should think about them, human beings that you should care for them?" (Psalm 8:4 NLT).

When you're talking to God, pay attention to what you're saying. Ask Him to unskew your thoughts and prayers.

*Thank You, Lord, for watching over me!*

## PRAYER JAR INSPIRATION:
*My God cares for me!*

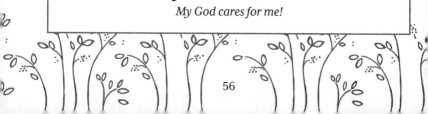

# SKEWED PRAYERS: PART 2

*If I have sinned, what [harm] have I done You, O You Watcher*
*and Keeper of men? Why have You set me as a mark for You,*
*so that I am a burden to myself [and You]? And why do You*
*not pardon my transgression and take away my iniquity?*
*For now shall I lie down in the dust; and [even if] You will*
*seek me diligently, [it will be too late, for] I shall not be.*
JOB 7:20-21 AMPC

Job's prayer goes even more haywire, so consumed is he by pain and sorrow. He's lost everything except his wife. . .whose only suggestion to him was to curse God and die.

Now Job is lashing out at God, thinking all this calamity may be due to some sin he'd committed, which is what his three friends have suggested. He's so depressed that he's not only lost hope but is expecting—and perhaps even looking forward to—his death.

Perhaps you're in Job's shoes (if he had any left!). Maybe your loss has led you into false thinking and skewed prayers. If so, remember that God is your Watcher and Keeper. Even though you may have sinned, He still watches over you to make sure you're okay. He's still providing for you, forgiving you, and gently leading you.

*No matter what comes against me, Lord,*
*help me to never go against You!*

## PRAYER JAR INSPIRATION:

*My God watches over me with love and forgiveness!*

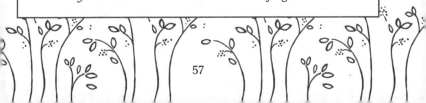

# SPIRITUAL EARS AND EYES

*Then Job said to the Lord, I know that You can do all things, and that
no thought or purpose of Yours can be restrained or thwarted. . . .
[I now see] I have [rashly] uttered what I did not understand, things too
wonderful for me, which I did not know. . . . I had heard of You [only]
by the hearing of the ear, but now my [spiritual] eye sees You. Therefore
I loathe [my words] and abhor myself and repent in dust and ashes.*

JOB 42:1-3, 5-6 AMPC

After an intense conversation with the Lord, Job finally gets his head
straight. He realizes that God's purpose stands above all things. That
no matter what happens in our lives, His will cannot be restrained.
That there will always be so many things we neither understand nor
know about God's methods.

Like Job, we sometimes don't exactly get the gist of what God
is saying. Sometimes we don't understand what He's doing. During
these times, we must hear and see with our spiritual ears and eyes. We
need to trust that God has only good in store for us. And we must
apologize to Him when we get things wrong.

*Thank You, Lord, for loving me even when I get things wrong!*

## PRAYER JAR INSPIRATION:

*Lord, help me hear and see with spiritual ears and eyes!*

# HONEST TO GOD

*"So here's what you must do. Take seven bulls and seven rams,
and go to my friend Job. Sacrifice a burnt offering on your own
behalf. My friend Job will pray for you, and I will accept his prayer.
He will ask me not to treat you as you deserve for talking nonsense
about me, and for not being honest with me, as he has."*

JOB 42:8 MSG

Job's friends—Eliphaz, Bildad, and Zophar—had gone to visit Job when he was engulfed in grief and loss. In their conversations, they misrepresented God to him, concluding that Job must've done something horribly wrong for God to have sent him such calamities.

Minister and author, Matthew Henry, wrote, "The devil had undertaken to prove Job a hypocrite, and his three friends had condemned him as a wicked man. . . . Job's friends had wronged God, by making prosperity a mark of the true church, and affliction a certain proof of God's wrath."

For Job's friends to become right with God, God required a sacrifice from them and a prayer of forgiveness from Job. Only then would God remove their punishment and forgive.

Your sins, your wrong thinking, may bring grief and consequences to yourself and others. But no matter what happens, God will never treat you as you deserve—He's always ready to forgive.

*Lord, may I always be willing to pray for the forgiveness of a friend.*

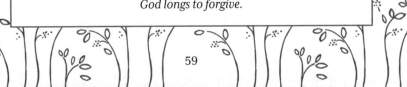

## PRAYER JAR INSPIRATION:

*God longs to forgive.*

# OFFERING UP

*Unto You, O Lord, do I bring my life. O my God, I trust, lean on, rely on, and am confident in You. . . . Remember, O Lord, Your tender mercy and loving-kindness; for they have been ever from of old.*

PSALM 25:1-2, 6 AMPC

When we're looking to God and seeking His forgiveness, we often have trouble finding the words to say. That's when we can look to the psalms for help.

Psalm 25 has the perfect opening: "Unto You, O Lord, do I bring my life." These words tell God that you're bringing your entire self into His presence. You're offering Him not just your mind, heart, soul, spirit, and body but your past, present, and future.

The next sentence is a reminder of what God means to you—how much you can lean on Him and trust His promises. Lastly, the passage says you can find assurance by remembering His unchanging mercy, gentleness, and loving-kindness.

Allow these words to linger in your mind. If they don't strike a chord within you, check out a different translation of the Bible or another psalm. Work with them until they feel personal. Then, in your petition for God's forgiveness, offer up your whole life to God, knowing He is—and always will be—the Lord of forgiveness.

*"Unto You, O Lord, do I bring my life."*

## PRAYER JAR INSPIRATION:
*I trust and rest in God's mercy.*

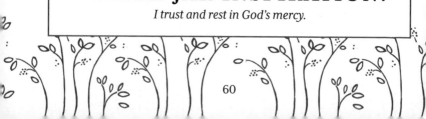

# YOUTHFUL INDISCRETIONS

*Remember not the sins (the lapses and frailties) of my youth or my transgressions; according to Your mercy and steadfast love remember me, for Your goodness' sake, O Lord. Good and upright is the Lord; therefore will He instruct sinners in [His] way. He leads the humble in what is right, and the humble He teaches His way.*

PSALM 25:7-9 AMPC

We all have a history. Some things you might look back on with humble pride; others you might shudder to think about or admit to God. But everything you've done has made you the woman you are today—a woman seeking God's love, guidance, and forgiveness.

Once again, the psalms come to your aid in helping you find the right words—this time for a prayer of repentance over a not-so-upright past. To help your past become the past, you must own up to the missteps you made in your youth. With today's verses, you can ask God to *forget* about your past misdeeds. . .while at the same time asking Him to deal with you in the light of His love and mercy and instruct you in the way you should go.

*Lord, please forget the missteps I made when I was young.*

## PRAYER JAR INSPIRATION:

*God, forgive and forget my prior missteps. Teach me to walk rightly.*

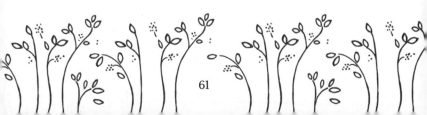

# LIVE IN GOODNESS

*O LORD, the Eternal, bring glory to Your name, and forgive my sins because they are beyond number. MAY anyone who fears the Eternal be shown the path he should choose. His soul will NOT only live in goodness, but his children will inherit the land.*

PSALM 25:11-13 VOICE

Preceding these verses, the psalmist asks God to teach him His ways and feed him His Word. Why? "Because You are the True God who has saved me," he writes. "I wait all day long, hoping, trusting in You" (verse 5 VOICE). It's clear this petitioner is very familiar with God. Yet along with his devotion to the Lord, he feels the overwhelming sense of sin in his life. He knows he needs God's pardon for the countless wrongs he has done.

Have you ever tried to list all the ways you've stumbled in your life? Perhaps yours would also be numerous. But thankfully, you belong to a God who is more than ready to forgive those who come to Him and ask. And He will make clear which direction you should go in your walk with Him. Why? Because He, like you, wants you to live your best life in Him.

*Thank You, Lord, for forgiving my numerous sins. Show me which way to go and how to live a good life in You.*

## PRAYER JAR INSPIRATION:

*With God's help, my soul will only live in goodness!*

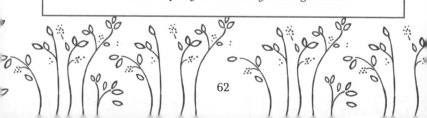

# HOPE IN GOD

*Turn to me and have mercy, for I am alone and in deep distress.*
*My problems go from bad to worse. Oh, save me from them all!*
*Feel my pain and see my trouble. Forgive all my sins. . . . May*
*integrity and honesty protect me, for I put my hope in you.*

PSALM 25:16-18, 21 NLT

When the world feels like it's caving in on you, when you feel as if you're all alone, when all you want to do is sit down and cry, go to God. Tell Him exactly how you feel. Tell Him everything that's going on in your world, knowing that Jesus can feel your pain. He can understand your trouble. He can sympathize with your struggles—because He Himself has been there.

Yet, there's one thing Jesus never knew: sin. That's why He could die to save you from yours. So don't hold back. Put it all out there for God. If you must, wallow in your pain for a little bit. But when you rise up, remember who is on your side—God the Creator, Protector, Refuge, All-Powerful. Put your hope in Him, and you will find strength to face your troubles. . .and the relief of forgiven sins!

*To You I turn, Lord. Hear my prayer! Save me*
*quickly! Forgive all! Be my hope!*

> # PRAYER JAR INSPIRATION:
> *My forgiveness and hope are found in my God!*

# HEALING OF THE INNER SOUL

*The Lord will sustain, refresh, and strengthen him on his bed
of languishing; all his bed You [O Lord] will turn, change, and
transform in his illness. I said, Lord, be merciful and gracious
to me; heal my inner self, for I have sinned against You.*

PSALM 41:3-4 AMPC

Sin is an offence against God. Anything you do that's contrary to
His plan is harmful not only to yourself and others but to Him. And
when you harm God, your soul feels it, prompting you to cry out to
the Father of forgiveness.

Sometimes, your soul sickness can even lead to physical maladies. So
when you find yourself feeling unwell—spiritually or physically—cry
out to God. Ask Him to transform your illness, to touch you with
His love, care, mercy, and forgiveness. Then rest easy, knowing that
God loves to bring transformation and healing, love and compassion,
mercy and forgiveness into your life and soul.

*Lord of mercy, forgive me for harming You, myself,
and others. Transform my weakness, my malady,
with Your grace, mercy, and strength.*

## PRAYER JAR INSPIRATION:

*Only God can transform me and heal my inner self!*

# EXCEPT THE LORD

*When it was time for my first defense, no one showed up to*
*support me. Everyone abandoned me (may it not be held*
*against them) except the Lord. He stood by me, strengthened*
*me, and backed the truth I proclaimed with power so it*
*may be heard by all the non-Jews. He rescued me.*

2 TIMOTHY 4:16-17 VOICE

Let's face it. People often disappoint us. We find ourselves counting
on them for love and support, but just when we need them the most,
they're nowhere to be found!

That's what happened to Paul. He had many friends in Rome, but
as it turned out, they didn't support him when he was on trial for his
life. Yet amazingly, despite their desertion, Paul knew fear was the
motivating factor, so he offered God his forgiveness for them.

What's even more wonderful is that the Lord remained by his
side through it all. God is a blessing within reach of all believers, even
those riddled with fear.

*Lord, may I be as merciful as You toward those who*
*have wronged me. Thank You for Your continual mercy*
*in my life and constant presence by my side!*

---

## PRAYER JAR INSPIRATION:

*"I know the Lord will continue to rescue me. . .and carry me*
*safely to His heavenly kingdom" (2 Timothy 4:18 VOICE).*

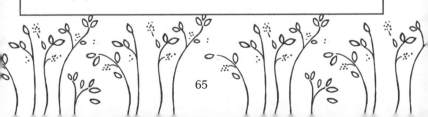

# HEARTFELT INTENT

*May your silver rot right along with you, Simon! To think the Holy*
*Spirit is some kind of magic that can be procured with money! You*
*aren't even close to being ready for this kind of ministry; your heart*
*is not right with God. You need to turn from your past, and you need*
*to pray that the Lord will forgive the evil intent of your heart.*

Acts 8:20-22 voice

Simon, a local sorcerer, had for years been amazing the people of
Samaria. Everyone there referred to him as "the Great One—the Power
of God" (Acts 8:10 NLT). But when the apostle Philip preached the
good news of Jesus Christ, many people—including Simon—were
baptized and began to follow Philip instead, awed by the miracles
he performed.

Then, when apostles Peter and John arrived in Samaria and prayed
for the new believers to receive the Holy Spirit, they did! Simon,
seeing this great power coming upon his fellow citizens, offered to
give the apostles money so that he could have the power to pass on
the Spirit as well. But Peter set him straight, telling him the Spirit is
not some magic trick that can be bought.

God knows your heart. He knows when your intent is evil. But if
you pray, He will forgive and help you turn your heart around.

*Help me, Lord, to keep my heart's intent pure.*

## PRAYER JAR INSPIRATION:
*May my heart's intentions always be good.*

# GOD HEARS YOUR PRAYER

*Come with great power, O God, and rescue me! Defend me with your might. Listen to my prayer, O God. Pay attention to my plea. . . . I took my troubles to the Lord; I cried out to him, and he answered my prayer.*

PSALM 54:1-2; 120:1 NLT

Know this, woman of God: the Lord hears your prayers. His eyes are constantly watching you. He even sends angels so that you won't trip. But if and when you do, His ears are open to your pleas. All you have to do is come to Him and pray for forgiveness.

If you do, you can be sure that even if you can't find the words, God will know what you are trying to say, what you are asking, what your soul and heart are feeling, what your spirit is craving, and what you need.

So, do not fear that the Lord doesn't hear. He is open to you, 24/7. All you need to do is lift up your heart and soul to Him. Give Him your plea for forgiveness, your request for guidance. And you will receive all!

*Hear my prayer, Lord, as I bring my sins,*
*my soul, and my troubles to You.*

## PRAYER JAR INSPIRATION:

*My God hears my prayers!*

# A NATIONAL REQUEST

*Do not hold the sins of our ancestors against us, but send Your*
*compassion to meet us quickly, God. We are in deep despair. Help*
*us, O God who saves us, to the honor and glory of Your name.*
*Pull us up, deliver us, and forgive our sins, for Your name's sake.*
*Don't give these people any reason to ask, "Where is their God?"*

PSALM 79:8-10 VOICE

There may come a time when we feel compelled to pray for our entire nation. A time when we feel as if we are being punished for the sins of those before us. A time when we wonder how we, a supposedly God-fearing nation, might appear in the eyes of outsiders as the enemy tramples us.

When our nation is under attack, we may experience shock, despair, and fear. We feel beaten down and unable to look anywhere but up. For we know that is where our help comes from.

Today, pray for your nation. Pray for not only its leaders but the common person who is just trying to live a godly life in the midst of societal upheaval. Pray that God's compassion, deliverance, and forgiveness shines down upon you and lifts you—and your nation—up.

*Lord, we've really messed things up. I pray You would,*
*in Your compassion, deliver and forgive our nation.*

## PRAYER JAR INSPIRATION:

*God, forgive this nation. Deliver us for Your name's sake!*

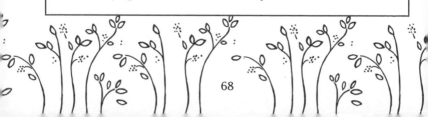

# ACCEPTING AND RECEIVING GOD'S FORGIVENESS

Of all our uncountable human needs, there is none greater than the need for God's forgiveness. The question is this: How do we accept and receive His forgiveness?

In Acts 3:19 (KJV), Peter spoke about the need for repentance: "Repent ye therefore, and be converted, that your sins may be blotted out, when the times of refreshing shall come from the presence of the Lord." And when the Philippian jailer asked Paul in Acts 16:30 what he must do to be saved, Paul answered in verse 31 (KJV): "Believe on the Lord Jesus Christ, and thou shalt be saved, and thy house."

To receive God's forgiveness, we must apologize for our sins and believe in the Lord Jesus Christ. We can be forgiven only when we ask for forgiveness and repent, putting our faith in the Lord.

What a wonderful gift God has given us! Don't you feel blessed knowing that in order to be forgiven, all you have to do is repent and believe?

# BOLDLY TO THE THRONE

*This High Priest of ours understands our weaknesses, for he faced
all of the same testings we do, yet he did not sin. So let us come
boldly to the throne of our gracious God. There we will receive his
mercy, and we will find grace to help us when we need it most.*

HEBREWS 4:15-16 NLT

How wonderful that Jesus came to save us! That He is our High Priest
who totally understands what we're going through—who knows and
is ready to supply whatever we need, whenever we need it!

So when you need help, when you stumble, when you are weak,
head to the throne of God's grace. Do so with all boldness, knowing
you will find the mercy, grace, and love you require—just when you
need it the most.

*Thank You, Lord, for understanding me and making
allowances for my weakness. May I run to You when
I need Your mercy. In Jesus' name, amen.*

---

## PRAYER JAR INSPIRATION:

*Because of Jesus' love and grace, I receive all the
mercy and grace I need, just when I need it!*

---

# WHITE AS SNOW

*Come on now, let's walk and talk; let's work this out. Your wrongdoings are bloodred, but they can turn as white as snow. Your sins are red like crimson, but they can be made clean again like new wool.*

ISAIAH 1:18 VOICE

Jesus has a knack for transformation. So once you've turned from your former ways, confessed your missteps to God, and asked for His mercy and forgiveness, you must accept that you've been cleansed. He's done something for you that you could've never accomplished yourself. And now, the stain of your mistake has been wiped away. You are now white as snow.

So, let the weight of your burden slide off your shoulders. Leave it at the bottom of the cross. Know you've been relieved of your wrongs. Although you may still have to suffer whatever consequences your error caused, you are fully cleansed in God's eyes! Do you see yourself cleansed in your own eyes?

*Help me, Lord Jesus, to understand that because of Your sacrifice for me, You made me squeaky clean the moment I confessed my sins and turned to You! For that, I praise and thank You!*

---

# PRAYER JAR INSPIRATION:

*Jesus' forgiveness makes me white as snow!*

---

# INTIMATE WITH GOD

*No longer will people have to teach each other or encourage their
family members and say, "You must know the Eternal." For all of
them will know Me intimately themselves—from the least to the
greatest of society. I will be merciful when they fail and forgive their
wrongs. I will never call to mind or mention their sins again.*

JEREMIAH 31:34 VOICE

Jesus came into this world especially for you. He knew you couldn't keep God's laws. So, Jesus did what nobody else could: He sacrificed His life so that you could live in an intimate relationship with God.

Perhaps you don't feel as close to God as you'd like. If so, take this opportunity to start your journey! First, immerse yourself in God's Word. Take His promises to heart. Learn of the overwhelming love Jesus has for you. Then, know that when you get things wrong, God will make them right—in your relationships, your life plans, your hopes, and your dreams. Know that He not only forgives but forgets your missteps. Simply believe!

*I want to be closer to You, Lord, to experience You more
when I'm in Your Word. Lead me the way You want me to go.
Help me know I have received Your forgiveness. Amen.*

## PRAYER JAR INSPIRATION:

*Jesus is my intimate Lord and Friend—
my passageway to God's presence!*

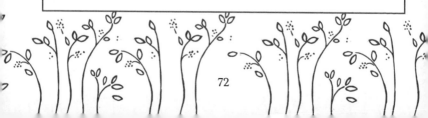

# MOST BLESSED WOMAN

*[Most] blessed is the man who believes in, trusts in, and relies
on the Lord, and whose hope and confidence the Lord is.
For he shall be like a tree planted by the waters that spreads out
its roots by the river; and it shall not see and fear when heat
comes; but its leaf shall be green. It shall not be anxious and full
of care in the year of drought, nor shall it cease yielding fruit.*

JEREMIAH 17:7-8 AMPC

God wants you to trust in Him for *everything*. He wants your hope
and confidence to be in Him. So, on those days that you feel like no
one—not even God—can forgive you, think again.

After confessing your missteps to God, don't allow your shame
to obscure His forgiveness. Instead, claim it! For when you do, you'll
find yourself opening up to Him about everything that's going on in
your life. You'll feel closer than ever to your Lord of forgiveness. And
you'll begin to see your life prosper. Even when circumstances turn
sour, you'll neither fear nor become anxious but find yourself at peace
with the God who loves you more than you'll ever know.

*Thank You, Lord, for forgiving me and loving me beyond all others.*

## PRAYER JAR INSPIRATION:

*My hope and confidence are in my Lord!*

# DARK HEART

*"The heart is hopelessly dark and deceitful, a puzzle that no one can figure out. But I, GOD, search the heart and examine the mind. I get to the heart of the human. I get to the root of things. I treat them as they really are, not as they pretend to be."*

JEREMIAH 17:9-10 MSG

You've asked God for forgiveness. You've read all the Bible passages, talked to some other Christian friends, and even consulted with your pastor. And still your heart is sending you false signals, trying to convince you there must be something else you must say, some deed you must perform before you can be fully forgiven.

This is when you need to stop listening to your heart and start believing God's Word. Instead of letting your heart boss you around, go to God. Tell Him you're struggling with accepting His forgiveness. Ask Him to get to the root of the problem. Allow Him to search your heart and examine your mind—to heal you where you need healing, to search your inner darkness, and to bring out the light.

God will help you find the truth.

*Lord, search my heart. Examine my mind.*
*Bring me the light of Your forgiveness.*

## PRAYER JAR INSPIRATION:

*My God is my beacon of light.*

# RELEASING THE ENTIRE BURDEN

*Cast your burden on the Lord [releasing the weight of it]*
*and He will sustain you; He will never allow the [consistently]*
*righteous to be moved (made to slip, fall, or fail). . . .*
*I will trust in, lean on, and confidently rely on You.*

PSALM 55:22-23 AMPC

You've asked God for forgiveness, and you believe He has given it to you. But some questions still remain, niggling at the edges of your mind and heart.

This is when you want to spend some quality time with God, asking Him to help you get to the root of the matter. For until you confess all, totally unburdening your mind and heart to God, you won't have the confidence to press on. And when you're not spiritually strong, you're more likely to fail again.

So, find some time to spend with God—time beyond your daily devotions. Ask Him to sustain you and to help you release your entire burden. Once all is off your chest and forgiven, nothing in the world can shake you!

*Lord, help me cast all of my burden upon You,*
*confident that You will forgive all.*

## PRAYER JAR INSPIRATION:

*God can bear the weight of my sin—and forgive it!*

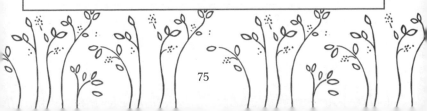

# TURN AROUND

*God fulfilled what He foretold. . . , that His Christ (the Messiah)*
*should undergo ill treatment and be afflicted and suffer. So repent*
*(change your mind and purpose); turn around and return [to*
*God], that your sins may be erased (blotted out, wiped clean),*
*that times of refreshing (of recovering from the effects of heat,*
*of reviving with fresh air) may come from the presence of the Lord.*
ACTS 3:18-19 AMPC

God's intense, profound, and abundant love for you prompted Him to allow His Son to be sacrificed on your behalf so that your sins could be forgiven. There's no way you can repay that sacrifice—but what you *can* do is walk God's way the best you can and confess your missteps along the way.

Yet there's one more box to check, one more task to take up: to turn around from your old path. To change the way you've been living your life. To perhaps even rethink your goals. If you don't have any goals, perhaps turning around means living more intentionally for God.

The point is that once you've been forgiven, repentance is necessary. From what path might you need to turn?

*Help me, Lord, to turn from the path that caused me to*
*stumble. I want to walk more closely with You.*

## PRAYER JAR INSPIRATION:

*Lord, show me how to turn around my life for You.*

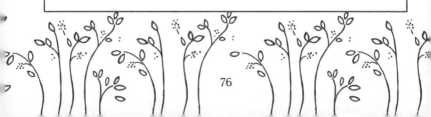

# WHO HAS NOT SINNED?

*Jesus: Let the first stone be thrown by the one
among you who has not sinned.*

JOHN 8:7 VOICE

Deciding to test Jesus, the scribes and Pharisees brought a woman before Him. The Pharisees said she'd been caught in the act of adultery. Under the law of Moses, such a woman was to be killed by stoning. "What do You say about it?" they asked (John 8:5 VOICE).

Jesus started writing something in the dirt, and then He stood up and said, "Let the first stone be thrown by the one among you who has not sinned" (John 8:7 VOICE). Jesus then bent down and began writing with His finger in the dirt again.

At first, the Pharisees just stood there. Then, one by one, they began to leave—beginning with the older (and presumably wiser) men.

Jesus wants you to know you're not the only one who sins. That sounds obvious, but when we're plagued by guilt, we sometimes need this reminder. Not that we should be cavalier about our sins or God's forgiveness. That wouldn't be healthy for anyone. But sometimes, we do need to remember that what God has washed away will stay washed away. There's no need to keep worrying if you've been forgiven or not. You have. Now it's time to move on to a brighter future!

*Thank You, Lord, for Your forgiveness. Help me accept it and move on.*

## PRAYER JAR INSPIRATION:

*All sin. But all who ask are forgiven. Thank You, Lord!*

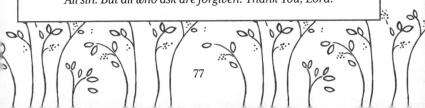

# ALL HE ASKS

*Jesus: Dear woman, where is everyone? Are we alone?*
*Did no one step forward to condemn you?*
**Woman Caught in Adultery:** *Lord, no one has condemned me.*
*Jesus: Well, I do not condemn you either; all I ask is that you*
*go and from now on avoid the sins that plague you.*

JOHN 8:10-11 VOICE

The Pharisees had brought to Jesus a woman who'd been caught in adultery. They were trying to trip Him up, to see if He would disagree with Moses' law. But when Jesus told them that whoever had not sinned could throw the first stone, the Pharisees walked away one by one.

When they were alone, Jesus lovingly addressed the woman as "dear." Then He asked questions to which He already knew the answers: "Where is everyone? . . . Did no one step forward to condemn you?" She said no one had. Then, He who was without sin also refused to condemn her. Instead, He merely advised her to go on her way and stop living in sin.

Jesus says the same to you. You've asked for forgiveness, so believe you've received it! Don't get hung up thinking everyone but you is perfect. Instead, accept God's forgiveness. And live the rest of your life avoiding the temptation that led you to err. That's all He asks.

*Give me the strength, Lord, to avoid the sins for which I've*
*asked forgiveness and to live the rest of my life in You.*

## PRAYER JAR INSPIRATION:

*Lord, help me do all You ask.*

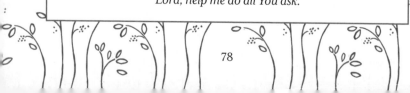

# THE WEEPING WOMAN: PART 1

*Just as Jesus enters the man's home and takes His place at the table,
a woman from the city—notorious as a woman of ill repute—follows Him
in. She has heard that Jesus will be at the Pharisee's home, so she comes
in and approaches Him, carrying an alabaster flask of perfumed oil.*

LUKE 7:36-37 VOICE

A Pharisee has invited Jesus to dine with him at his house. Jesus, taking the religious leader up on his offer, reclines at the Pharisee's table. Just then, a former prostitute, having heard Jesus was going to be there, comes in with a very expensive flask of perfume. Seeing Jesus, she begins to cry, letting her tears fall on Jesus' feet.

The Son of God does not turn her away. He does not cringe, pulling His feet away from her. Instead, He lovingly watches as she pours her love out to the One who forgives all.

You have confessed your sins to the same gentle Savior. You have been forgiven too. Know that Jesus still loves you and welcomes you into His presence. Accept what He offers, knowing you'll always have His love.

*Jesus, thank You for forgiving me. Help me accept that forgiveness,
knowing I am always welcome in Your loving presence.*

## PRAYER JAR INSPIRATION:
*Jesus, Your abundant love and forgiveness
lead me to love You all the more.*

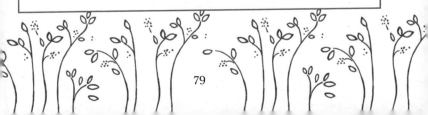

# THE WEEPING WOMAN: PART 2

*Then she begins to cry, she kneels down so her tears fall on Jesus'*
*feet, and she starts wiping His feet with her own hair. Then she*
*actually kisses His feet, and she pours the perfumed oil on them.*

LUKE 7:38 VOICE

Imagine being a strict adherent to Moses' law. On the scene comes this young upstart named Jesus, whom you've invited to dinner. Just as your guest takes His place at your table, a former prostitute comes into your home carrying a flask. She begins crying, letting her tears fall on Jesus' feet and then wiping His tear-covered feet with her hair. Now she's kissing His feet and covering them with expensive perfume—which she probably purchased with her ill-gotten gains!

You begin thinking, *"Now I know this guy is a fraud. If He were a real prophet, He would have known this woman is a sinner and He would never let her get near Him, much less touch Him. . .or kiss Him!"* (Luke 7:39 VOICE).

Always remember that when you've confessed your sins, you're forgiven. Never let others' opinions of you keep you from expressing your joy at such forgiveness. The only thoughts or opinions you should be concerned about are God's. In His eyes, you are loved and absolved!

*The only opinion I care about is Yours, Jesus!*
*Thank You for forgiving me!*

## PRAYER JAR INSPIRATION:

*I have joy in Jesus' forgiveness!*

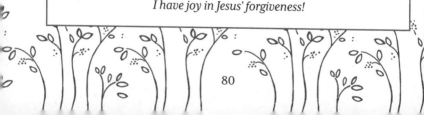

# THE WEEPING WOMAN: PART 3

*When the Pharisee who had invited him saw this, he said to himself,*
*"If this man were a prophet, he would know what kind of woman*
*is touching him. She's a sinner!" Then Jesus answered his thoughts.*
*"Simon," he said to the Pharisee, "I have something to say to you."*

LUKE 7:39-40 NLT

As the woman of ill-repute rubs Jesus' feet with her tears, perfume, and hair—and kisses His feet with her lips—Jesus tells His host, Simon the Pharisee, a parable.

A money lender had two customers: one owed him five hundred pieces of silver and the other fifty. Neither could repay him. So, he forgave them both, wiping their debts off his books. Jesus asked the Pharisee who he thought would love the lender more. Simon replied, "The one who was forgiven more" (Luke 7:43 VOICE).

Jesus commended Simon for his answer. Then, He pointed out that Simon had neither washed Jesus' feet nor given Him a kiss of greeting nor offered Him oil to refresh Himself. Yet, this woman had done all three. She who was forgiven much, loves much.

What love will you show your Master today?

*Thank You, Lord, for being so forgiving. May I love You all the more!*

---

## PRAYER JAR INSPIRATION:

*Lord, I love You more than I can say!*

---

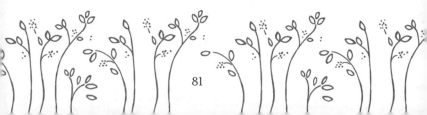

# THE WEEPING WOMAN: PART 4

*And He said to her, Your sins are forgiven! . . . Your faith
has saved you; go (enter) into peace [in freedom from all
the distresses that are experienced as the result of sin].*

LUKE 7:48, 50 AMPC

Jesus knew the secrets of the weeping woman's soul. He knew what
she'd experienced. . .and what she was feeling in that moment, being
judged as she lovingly catered to the Lord of forgiveness. Jesus knew
she had received and rejoiced in her free forgiveness.

Jesus' parable of the lender forced Simon, the judgmental Pharisee,
to admit that the greater the sin forgiven, the more love the penitent
will have for the one who forgives.

Because of her faith that she had indeed been forgiven, Jesus wanted
this woman to know beyond doubt that she was free to experience the
peace that only He can provide. And now that she'd received it, she was
permitted to go and point others to Jesus, the source of her change.

You, too, have been changed by Jesus. Let others know!

*You, Lord, have been a life-changer for me! May other
people see how much Your forgiveness has changed me!*

## PRAYER JAR INSPIRATION:

*My faith not only saves me but also leads me into peace.*

# HIGH-POWERED
# DEFENSE LAWYER

*I am writing these things to help you avoid sin. If, however,*
*any believer does sin, we have a high-powered defense lawyer—*
*Jesus the Anointed, the righteous—arguing on our behalf before the*
*Father. It was through His sacrificial death that our sins were atoned.*
*But He did not stop there—He died for the sins of the whole world.*

1 JOHN 2:1-2 VOICE

The disciple John wrote to early Christians, hoping his letter would help them stay away from sin. Even so, he also told them that if they said they didn't sin, they were lying!

But John then reminded them that whenever they fell short, they'd have a wonderfully powerful advocate to represent them before the Father: Jesus, the One who never sinned.

How blessed can we be? Jesus not only died on our behalf to restore our relationship with our Creator, but He *continues* to defend us, even today!

Today and every day, remember that Jesus, your sinless Savior, has died for your sins and continues to defend you before God the Father when you mess up. Jesus has gone to great lengths to make you right with God. Praise His name!

*Thank You, Jesus, for continually rescuing me!*

## PRAYER JAR INSPIRATION:

*My life is blessed by Jesus!*

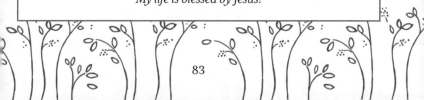

# PETER'S WEAKNESS

*This very night, before the cock crows in the*
*morning, you will deny Me three times.*
MATTHEW 26:34 VOICE

During the Last Supper, Peter had emphatically told Jesus, "Lord, maybe everyone else will trip and fall tonight, but I will not. I'll be beside You. I won't falter" (Matthew 26:33 VOICE). Jesus disagreed. . .and told Peter so. Still, Peter denied Jesus' prediction.

Later that same night, Jesus went with the disciples to the garden of Gethsemane. He told them to sit down while He went to pray. Taking with Him Peter, James, and John, Jesus told the trio to stay awake while He went a little farther.

In great agony, Jesus met with God in prayer. And every time He went back to see how the three were doing, He noticed Peter had fallen asleep. Jesus told him, "The spirit is willing, but the body is weak. Watch and pray and take care that you are not pulled down during a time of testing" (Matthew 26:41 VOICE).

Just like Jesus knew Peter's weakness, He knows yours. And just as He was later able to forgive Peter, He forgives you. Your job is simply to accept His forgiveness—and to stay awake so that you, too, are not pulled into sin.

*Thank You, Lord, for Your continuous compassion and understanding.*

## PRAYER JAR INSPIRATION:

*Lord, help me to stay alert and prayerful so*
*that I will be strong amid testing.*

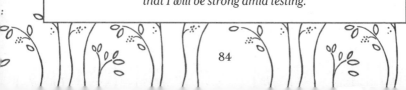

# PETER'S FEAR

*When they saw the armed crowd take Jesus into custody,*
*the disciples fled. . . . Peter followed, at a safe distance, all the way*
*into the courtyard of the high priest, and he sat down with the guards*
*to warm himself at their fire. He hoped no one would notice.*

MARK 14:50, 54 VOICE

For all his bravado on the night of Jesus' arrest, Peter was only human. Although he'd promised to stay by Jesus' side no matter what, he still turned tail and ran. Later, he followed at a safe distance, curious about Jesus' fate.

As Peter waited outside the high priest's courtyard, warming himself by a fire, someone recognized him as one of Jesus' followers. And Peter denied it. This happened three times. . .and all three times, Peter denied knowing Jesus. Suddenly, the cock crowed for the third time, just as Jesus had predicted (Mark 14:66-72), leaving Peter in tears.

We, too, may sin out of weakness or fear. We, too, may weep tears of shame. But we must remember: Jesus can work with us—where we are and as we are. He's there at every turn.

*Forgive my weakness and fears, Lord. Help me*
*become stronger and take courage in You.*

## PRAYER JAR INSPIRATION:
*Jesus meets me where I am, as I am!*

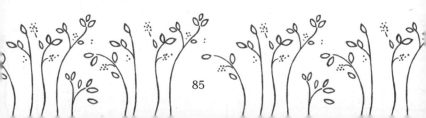

# THE PURPOSE OF PETER'S PREDICAMENT

*"Simon, stay on your toes. Satan has tried his best to separate all of you from me, like chaff from wheat. Simon, I've prayed for you in particular that you not give in or give out. When you have come through the time of testing, turn to your companions and give them a fresh start."*

LUKE 22:31-32 MSG

Peter boasted to Jesus that he'd never betray Him. That even if all the others fled, Peter would stick to Him like glue. But Jesus knew who Peter truly was—how far he'd come and how much further he had to go. In fact, Jesus had told him, "And now I'm going to tell you who you are, really are. You are Peter, a rock. This is the rock on which I will put together my church" (Matthew 16:17-18 MSG).

At any point in time, Jesus could've worked a miracle to help Peter succeed, to protect him from being tempted into weakness. But Jesus had a plan. And that plan was to help Peter become whom Jesus needed him to be. And he did!

When you slip up, remember failure is not fatal. Jesus will forgive as God slowly transforms you into the woman you were always meant to be.

*Thank You, Jesus, for reminding me that in Your eyes, failure is not fatal.*

## PRAYER JAR INSPIRATION:

*Jesus forgives as I endeavor to become the woman He created me to be!*

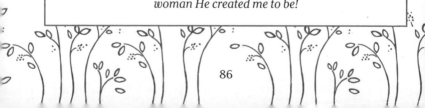

86

# THE MIRACLE OF FORGIVENESS

*Peter was hurt because He asked him the same*
*question a third time, "Do you love Me?"*
**Simon Peter:** *Lord, You know everything!*
*You know that I love You.*
**Jesus:** *Look after My sheep.*
JOHN 21:17 VOICE

After His resurrection, Jesus meets up with the disciples for a third time. In this scene, the men are fishing and have caught nothing. Jesus, seeing them from shore, suggests they try casting their nets in another location. They do. . .and their nets soon overflow with fish! Recognizing Jesus, the men hurry to shore.

After breakfast, Jesus asks Peter three times if he loves Him. Three times—the same number of times he denied knowing Jesus—Peter answers, "Yes! I love You, Lord!" And three times, Jesus tells Peter he is to serve as a leader in ministry, which he does very well.

About these verses, The Voice comments, "The disciples all learn a lesson that day. No matter what someone may have done, the Master wants the miracle of forgiveness to restore that person to be whom He made and called him or her to be." Words to soak in and remember.

*Lord, thank You for the miracle of forgiveness!*

## PRAYER JAR INSPIRATION:

*Jesus restores me to the person whom He*
*made me and called me to be!*

# ATTENTION PLEASE!

*Saul was [not only] consenting to [Stephen's] death [he was pleased and entirely approving]. . . . Saul shamefully treated and laid waste the church continuously [with cruelty and violence]; and entering house after house, he dragged out men and women and committed them to prison.*

ACTS 8:1, 3 AMPC

Before he became the apostle Paul, Saul of Tarsus was a "fuming, raging, hateful man who wanted to kill every last one of the Lord's disciples" (Acts 9:1 VOICE). But then Jesus got Saul's attention by literally stopping him in his tracks.

One day, when Saul was traveling to Damascus, a light from heaven flashed around him, bringing him to the ground. He then heard Jesus saying, "Saul, Saul, why are you attacking Me?" (Acts 9:4 VOICE). Jesus ordered Saul to get up, go into the city, and wait for further instructions. Now blinded, Saul was led by his speechless traveling companions into Damascus.

When we've gone too far, when our malicious missteps are too much for the Lord, He calls our attention to our mistake.

To what might the Lord be drawing your attention?

*Draw attention to areas in my life that aren't pleasing to You, Lord. Show me how to change my ways.*

## PRAYER JAR INSPIRATION:

*Lord, show me where I may be walking out of Your will.*

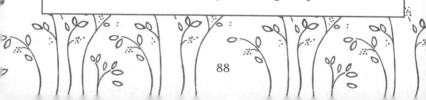

# "BUT LORD!"

*Now there was a believer in Damascus named Ananias.*
*The Lord spoke to him in a vision, calling, "Ananias!"*

ACTS 9:10 NLT

While Saul was in Damascus, awaiting further instructions from Jesus, the Lord spoke to a man named Ananias. He told him to go to Straight Street, where Saul of Tarsus was praying to Jesus at that exact moment! Jesus told Ananias He was showing Saul a vision of Ananias laying hands on him to restore his sight.

"But Lord," Ananias exclaimed, "I've heard about the horrible things this guy has done to believers in Jerusalem. He's authorized by the chief priests to arrest anyone who calls on Your name!"

Jesus said, "Go, for Saul is my chosen instrument to take my message to the Gentiles and to kings, as well as to the people of Israel" (Acts 9:15 NLT). And off Ananias went, ready to do as Jesus asked.

Jesus doesn't need to hear from us the sins someone else has committed. He knows. And if Jesus forgives someone, we need to do the same. He expects us to render good for evil, blessing for cursing, prayer for persecution. Why? Because God has a plan for all.

*Give me the wisdom, Lord, to forgive where You forgive—*
*to render good for evil wherever You please.*

---

## PRAYER JAR INSPIRATION:

*With God's strength, I will strive to forgive those whom He forgives.*

---

# IN GOD'S WILL

*So Ananias went and found Saul. He laid his hands on him
and said, "Brother Saul, the Lord Jesus, who appeared
to you on the road, has sent me so that you might regain
your sight and be filled with the Holy Spirit."*

ACTS 9:17 NLT

In obedience to Jesus, Ananias went to Straight Street and found
Saul there. Ananias was so trusting of Jesus that he addressed Saul,
this persecutor of Christian believers, as his brother!

After explaining why he was there, Ananias laid his hands on Saul
and prayed over him. Instantly, something like scales fell from Saul's
eyes. . .and he could see again! He then got up, and Ananias baptized
him. Afterward, he ate some food and regained his strength.

Saul then caused a sensation: this persecutor of Christians was
now hanging out with them and proclaiming in the temples that
Jesus was the Son of God!

There's no one Jesus can't transform into someone good. And when
we follow His commands by accepting His forgiveness of others—no
matter what they may have done—miracles begin to take place. We
start seeing God on the move through us and others.

Whom do you need to finally forgive today?

*Lord, reveal to me anyone whom You've forgiven—and whom I still
need to forgive—so that I can make room for You to work a miracle.*

## PRAYER JAR INSPIRATION:

*In God's will, I find my way!*

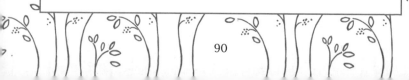

# ROOM FOR CHANGE

*Change your life, not just your clothes. Come back to GOD, your*
*God. And here's why: God is kind and merciful. He takes a deep*
*breath, puts up with a lot, this most patient God, extravagant in*
*love, always ready to cancel catastrophe. Who knows? Maybe he'll*
*do it now, maybe he'll turn around and show pity. Maybe, when all's*
*said and done, there'll be blessings full and robust for your GOD!*

JOEL 2:13 MSG

As we've seen with Saul the persecutor who became Paul the preacher, God goes to great lengths to forgive us and help us become what He originally designed us to be. But with that forgiveness must come a change of heart.

Saul's change was so drastic that he began to preach Jesus at the same place he'd planned to persecute Christians!

Your God is very patient with you. He puts up with a lot. So, don't be afraid to tell Him all that's going on in your life. No matter how much you've transgressed His command to love Him and others, He will not only forgive you but will find a way to change your situation into a blessing—just as He did for Saul.

*Lord, I need to get a few things off my chest. . . .*

## PRAYER JAR INSPIRATION:

*God, strengthen me as I accept Your forgiveness.*
*Help me find room for change!*

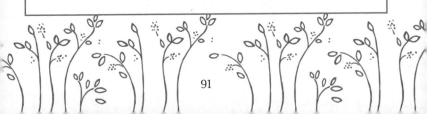

# MOVING FORWARD IN GOD

*If God hadn't been there for me, I never would have made it.*
*The minute I said, "I'm slipping, I'm falling," your love, God,*
*took hold and held me fast. When I was upset and beside*
*myself, you calmed me down and cheered me up.*

PSALM 94:17-19 MSG

There may be days when you doubt God has truly forgiven you. That's when you need to look into His Word once more. His truth will keep you from slipping back into your old ways—the one direction God doesn't want you to go.

Perhaps there's a certain sin for which you're not sure God has forgiven you: not taking care of yourself when you were pregnant, gossiping, saying hateful words, etc.

These are all lies, planted in your mind by the father of lies. So take confidence. Know that God does forgive and that He's always waiting to steer you back onto His track. Remember that God has a hold on you—and He'll never, ever let you go. Why? Because He loves you more than you can ever imagine. You have a place in His plan.

Today, know God is always there for you. His love will keep you close and calm.

*You know what I've done, Lord. Help me move forward in a new way!*

---

# PRAYER JAR INSPIRATION:

*In God, I trust that I can (and will) move forward.*

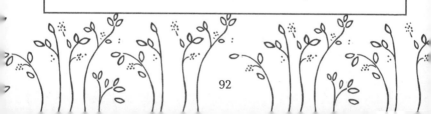

# BELIEVING PRAYER

*Are you hurting? Pray. Do you feel great? Sing. Are you sick? Call the*
*church leaders together to pray and anoint you with oil in the name of*
*the Master. Believing-prayer will heal you, and Jesus will put you on*
*your feet. And if you've sinned, you'll be forgiven—healed inside and out.*

JAMES 5:13-15 MSG

God's Word reminds us that, sometimes, it's best to pray for ourselves
in a group setting, not alone. The more believing hearts that are gathered together, the better.

We're encouraged to pray when we're hurting and to sing praises
when we're feeling great. In times of illness, it may be the anxiety
of an unconfessed sin that's keeping us down. Perhaps we want to
get a few things off our chest so that we can feel the peace of God's
forgiveness inside and out. Or maybe we've confessed to God but,
for some reason, don't feel as if we've been forgiven.

Whichever scenario applies to you, take your faith to fellow believers. Ask them to pray with you. Then do so, knowing you'll be forgiven.

*Increase my faith, Lord, as I pray with fellow*
*believers, seeking Your forgiveness.*

## PRAYER JAR INSPIRATION:

*Believing prayer brings results—praise God!*

# THROUGH THIS MAN

*So let it be clearly known and understood by you, brethren, that
through this Man forgiveness and removal of sins is now proclaimed to
you; and that through Him everyone who believes [who acknowledges
Jesus as his Savior and devotes himself to Him] is absolved (cleared
and freed) from every charge from which he could not be justified
and freed by the Law of Moses and given right standing with God.*

ACTS 13:38-39 AMPC

Jesus has thrown you a lifeline. He is the one Man whose death cleansed
you of sins. If you believe in Him, acknowledge Him as your Savior, and
dedicate your life to Him, you will be cleared of any misdeeds that have
stained your record.

There's no way anyone can get through this life without erring.
But whether your misstep was intentional or unintentional, God will
forgive you through Jesus. No ifs, ands, or buts about it.

Whenever your thoughts spiral out of control, head to Jesus or dive
into His Word. Take to heart the fact that you are a free woman who's
been cleared of all charges against her. Then offer your praise to God!

*Thank You, Lord, for removing my sins—
for absolving me of every charge!*

## PRAYER JAR INSPIRATION:

*In Jesus, I am free indeed!*

# ALL RIGHT

*For everyone has sinned; we all fall short of God's glorious standard.*
*Yet God, in his grace, freely makes us right in his sight. He did this*
*through Christ Jesus when he freed us from the penalty for our sins.*

ROMANS 3:23-24 NLT

If you have sinned, don't think you're alone. It's a part of the human condition. There's no way we can always get things right. We've all fallen *way* short of the standard God set in Moses' Law.

But then came Jesus. Now we are right in God's eyes. Because the Man who knew no sin died for us, we can live in God again!

So, never allow yourself to think Jesus hasn't forgiven you for that time you spilled a friend's secrets. Or for those things you said to your husband—things you want to take back even though you're certain he was wrong. Whatever sin you're nursing because you're not sure you were ever forgiven, take it to Jesus. Confess it again and believe that you've been forgiven and freed.

You're all right in God's eyes!

*I know I often fall short, Lord. Nevertheless, I know You've*
*forgiven me. Help that truth sink into my heart.*

---

## PRAYER JAR INSPIRATION:

*Thank God for His grace!*

---

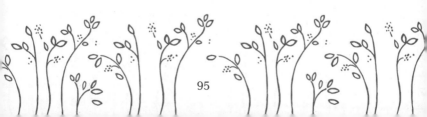

# SOMETHING TO THINK ABOUT

*Now it is rare to find someone willing to die for an upright person, although it's possible that someone may give up his life for one who is truly good. But think about this: while we were wasting our lives in sin, God revealed His powerful love to us in a tangible display—the Anointed One died for us.*

ROMANS 5:7-8 VOICE

Think about those people in your life who're closest to you. Who among them might you give your life for?

Perhaps it's your spouse. Your children. A sibling or a parent. Whomever it is, now imagine that this loved one has been living a wasteful life of sin. Would your love still be so great that you would die for that person?

That's a tough question. . .but not for Jesus. He loved people so much that before they even knew Him—while they were still entangled in sin and its consequences—Jesus died for them.

Today, think about Jesus' love for you. Praise Him for the amazing sacrifice He made on your behalf. Understand that you've already been freed from sin and will always be forgiven. You're a woman who's very much loved!

*Thank You, Lord, for Your powerful love. In You, I am so blessed.*

## PRAYER JAR INSPIRATION:

*God loves me in a powerful way!*

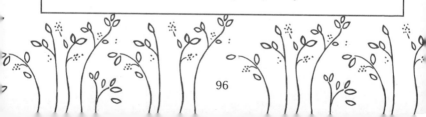

# CALLED TO FORGIVE OTHERS

In many ways, forgiveness is a learned behavior—we must learn how and why to forgive.

Did you know that an unwillingness to forgive someone can make you feel physically and spiritually ill? Some people hold on to their anger for decades, letting it control their thoughts and behavior. Grudges don't make people strong; they make them bitter. Forgiveness, however, has the power to heal *both* parties. In order to move on from past hurts, we must learn to forgive those who have harmed us and let it go. The Bible describes this as "turning the other cheek." It involves recognizing that you, too, are flawed and need forgiveness. . .and then treating others how you wish to be treated.

Failing to forgive will hurt us more than our offenders. If left unchecked, our bitterness will interfere with our emotional, physical, and spiritual wellbeing. But when we embrace unconditional forgiveness, we release all the pain we've bottled up inside. Even if we can't forget, we must learn to forgive. Otherwise, our heavenly Father will not forgive us.

"And be ye kind one to another, tenderhearted, forgiving one another, even as God for Christ's sake hath forgiven you" (Ephesians 4:32 KJV).

# WHY FORGIVE?

*Once Jesus was in a certain place praying. As he finished, one of
his disciples came to him and said, "Lord, teach us to pray."*

LUKE 11:1 NLT

Why should we forgive others? Because Jesus told us to. In fact, forgiveness was so important to Jesus that He made it an integral part of His model prayer!

The Lord's prayer begins with our request for God's name to be honored as holy. For His kingdom to come soon. For Him to provide for us each day. Then, we ask God to forgive us "as we forgive those who sin against us" (Luke 11:4 NLT). The final portion of the prayer requests God to lead us away from temptation.

When we look at this prayer, we see that God's forgiveness toward us depends on our forgiveness toward others! Until we no longer hold a grudge against someone who has wronged us, God's forgiveness will not come.

To whom do you need to extend forgiveness? Today is the perfect time to start! For as you forgive your fellow human, you will be forgiven by God. It doesn't get any plainer than that.

*I long for Your forgiveness, Lord. If I'm still holding back
forgiveness for someone, please bring that person to mind.
Then, give me the grace to extend mercy as You've done to me.*

## PRAYER JAR INSPIRATION:
*To be forgiven, I must forgive.*

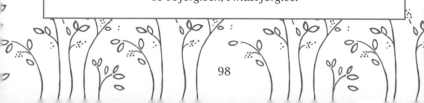

# GOING DEEPER

*For if you forgive people their trespasses [their reckless and willful*
*sins, leaving them, letting them go, and giving up resentment],*
*your heavenly Father will also forgive you. But if you do not*
*forgive others their trespasses [their reckless and willful sins,*
*leaving them, letting them go, and giving up resentment],*
*neither will your Father forgive you your trespasses.*

MATTHEW 6:14-15 AMPC

After giving His disciples a model for prayer, Jesus explained the forgiveness part more fully. (And the Amplified Classic Bible version helps us better understand what this forgiveness may entail.)

While our mouth might say we forgive someone, we may still hold on to some anger. In such cases, we haven't yet truly forgiven that individual.

Consider how you would feel if God didn't fully forgive you—if He just couldn't let go of something you did. Thankfully, God doesn't do things halfway. When He forgives, He does so fully. And that's what sets us free!

Whom might you need to forgive more fully?

*Lord, give me the strength to go deeper, to let go of all*
*grudges and resentments so that I—and the person*
*who has done me wrong—can be totally free.*

## PRAYER JAR INSPIRATION:

*I forgive others as God forgives me!*

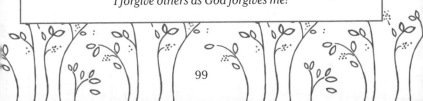

# BANISHING BITTERNESS

*Banish bitterness, rage and anger, shouting and slander, and any
and all malicious thoughts—these are poison. Instead, be kind
and compassionate. Graciously forgive one another just as God
has forgiven you through the Anointed, our Liberating King.*

EPHESIANS 4:31-32 VOICE

Some have said that refusing to forgive someone is like drinking
poison. . .and hoping the other person dies.

In his letter to the church in Ephesus, Paul addresses the kernel
of truth found in that idea by giving tips for how not to grieve God's
Holy Spirit. First on the list: banishing any sign of unforgiveness,
which can poison your life. These signs include bitterness, rage, anger,
evil gossip, and malicious and vengeful thoughts about someone.

Instead of dealing with the fruits of unforgiveness, try another
tactic by finding a way to repay evil with good. Be kind and compassionate to those who treat you badly. Forgive them, using the grace
with which God forgives you.

*Lord, help me always find a way to forgive those who have
wronged me, no matter how difficult it may seem.*

## PRAYER JAR INSPIRATION:

*God gives me the strength to graciously forgive others.*

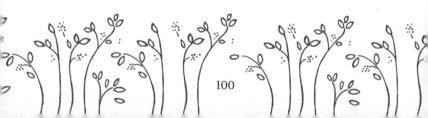

# LOVING WELL

*Love others well, and don't hide behind a mask; love authentically.*
*Despise evil; pursue what is good as if your life depends on it. Live in*
*true devotion to one another, loving each other as sisters and brothers.*

ROMANS 12:9-10 VOICE

Jesus made sure His followers knew the commandments that encompass all the laws of Moses and the prophets. The first and most important one is "You shall love the Lord your God with all your heart and with all your soul and with all your mind (intellect)" (Matthew 22:37 AMPC). The "second is like it: You shall love your neighbor as [you do] yourself" (Matthew 22:39 AMPC).

In other words, you are to love God and others well. And to love well, you must look past the ways others have wronged you. Your love and forgiveness must be real, just like God's is to you.

The greater the evil someone has committed against you, the harder it becomes to love and forgive. Yet, that's exactly what God asks you to do. And He never gives you a challenge you can't handle.

*Help me, Lord, to love others authentically, just as You*
*love all people. My aim is to follow Your commands.*

## PRAYER JAR INSPIRATION:

*May I love and forgive well!*

# ALWAYS SPEAK BLESSINGS

*If people mistreat or malign you, bless them. Always speak blessings, not curses. . . . Work toward unity, and live in harmony with one another.*

ROMANS 12:14, 16 VOICE

In his letter to the Romans, the apostle Paul delves even deeper into the idea of forgiveness. . .and what he asks can sometimes seem very difficult.

If people mistreat you or insult you, Paul says you are to bless them. In fact, you're not to ever let a curse pass your lips! This sounds very difficult, especially when you're in the heat of the moment and your flesh is itching to overrule your spirit. Yet, that's what you're called to do.

Perhaps there were times that Hannah (first wife to Elkanah) wanted to curse the fertile Peninnah (second wife to Elkanah) for how much she teased her about Hannah's inability to have a child (1 Samuel 1:7). Yet, even when Hannah was reduced to tears, we never read of her maligning Peninnah.

Blessing your enemies can get difficult. But God promises that with Him, all things are possible.

*Guard my thoughts and mouth, Lord. Help me to always speak blessings, never curses.*

## PRAYER JAR INSPIRATION:

*May my words always bless others, Lord!*

# MAKING PEACE

*Do not retaliate with evil, regardless of the evil brought against you.*
*Try to do what is good and right and honorable as agreed upon by*
*all people. If it is within your power, make peace with all people.*

ROMANS 12:17-18 VOICE

When we're insulted, maligned, or injured—physically, mentally, emotionally, etc.—our flesh would like nothing better than to reach out and strike the other person. But if we're to live by the Spirit, we must take the higher road.

We are to fight evil with good. To not retaliate but instead make peace with those who injure and insult us. This is what separates the godly from the ungodly.

This idea of not retaliating was first laid out by Jesus, who said we are to offer our left cheek if someone strikes our right. To give up our coat if someone takes our shirt (Matthew 5:39-40).

Not retaliating is hardly ever the easiest path to take. But it's all part of the forgiveness journey that God expects us not to forsake. If you know someone with whom you need to make peace, do everything within your power to make that happen. And let the rest go.

*Lord, give me the strength I need to not just forgive but*
*to repay evil with good and be at peace with all.*

## PRAYER JAR INSPIRATION:

*God will help me, peace by peace.*

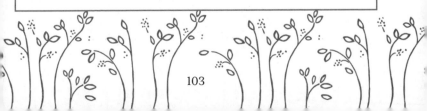

# GIVING IT TO GOD

*Don't insist on getting even; that's not for you to do. "I'll do*
*the judging," says God. "I'll take care of it." . . . Don't let evil*
*get the best of you; get the best of evil by doing good.*

ROMANS 12:19, 21 MSG

If you're still having trouble forgiving someone who wronged you
(whether intentionally or unintentionally)—if your flesh still wants
to get even—God allows you another route. Turn the problem over
to Him: He's the One who does the judging!

The last thing God wants you to do is let evil get the upper hand
in your life. So do yourself a favor and follow His advice. Leave all
the judging and avenging in *His* hands. By doing so, you'll be taking
a pill of blessedness instead of bitterness.

*Lord, there's one person I can't seem to forgive! Even worse, I want*
*revenge! But that's not how You want me to think or live. So, I leave that*
*person in Your hands, allowing You to take care of this situation for me.*

---

# PRAYER JAR INSPIRATION:

*I aim to get the best of evil by doing good!*

---

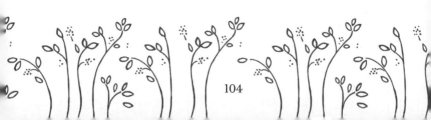

# WHEN IT'S PERSONAL

*"Be alert. If you see your friend going wrong, correct him.*
*If he responds, forgive him. Even if it's personal against you*
*and repeated seven times through the day, and seven times*
*he says, 'I'm sorry, I won't do it again,' forgive him."*

LUKE 17:3-4 MSG

Jesus makes it clear that we are to correct our friends if we see them going in the wrong direction (Luke 17:3). Then if our friends feel sorry for their mistake, we're to forgive them—even if what they did was personal.

Jesus tells us that even if we're injured seven times in one day, we should still let forgiveness take precedence. We shouldn't carry any resentment with us—the slate must be wiped clean!

Unbelievers who know nothing about Jesus' mandate may think this forgiving attitude makes us easy targets. But we are not of this world—never were, never will be. We are of the faith that forgives.

*Help me forgive, Lord, even when it's personal.*

---

## PRAYER JAR INSPIRATION:

*May I have the love to say, "I forgive you," even when it's personal.*

---

# FREELY FORGIVE

*Be gentle and forbearing with one another and, if one has a difference (a grievance or complaint) against another, readily pardoning each other; even as the Lord has [freely] forgiven you, so must you also [forgive].*

COLOSSIANS 3:13 AMPC

Even if we have a very good reason to be angry and resentful toward those who injure us, we are still to forgive. In fact, we're to harbor no ill will against those who have harmed us. We should be ready to repay their unkindness with our kindness. To do good to those who did us evil. To be willing to say, "I forgive you," when they ask for forgiveness. To treat the ones who injured us as if they had not.

This seems like a huge thing to ask. Yet, if we think about all the times God has forgiven us—all the times He's continued to love us no matter what—how could we not do the same for our fellow humans?

Every day, you will have a chance to forgive someone in your life, whether it be your husband, boyfriend, child, parents, in-laws, boss, teacher, or fellow Christians. You have a chance to be like Christ!

*Lord, help me freely forgive others. Help me be like You!*

## PRAYER JAR INSPIRATION:
*I will freely forgive—just as Jesus did!*

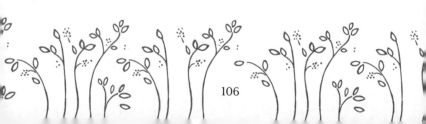

# BLESSING OF THE MERCIFUL

*Blessed (happy, to be envied, and spiritually prosperous—with life-joy and satisfaction in God's favor and salvation, regardless of their outward conditions) are the merciful, for they shall obtain mercy!*

MATTHEW 5:7 AMPC

In His Sermon on the Mount, Jesus went through His list of Beatitudes. And on that list was mercy. When you extend mercy to others, God will extend mercy to you!

Here's how the theologian Erasmus defined the merciful*:

[Those] who, through brotherly love, account another person's misery their own; who weep over the calamities of others; who, out of their own property, feed the hungry and clothe the naked; who admonish those that are in error, inform the ignorant, pardon the offending; and who, in short, use their utmost endeavours to relieve and comfort others.

That we are not perfect—that we all sin and fall short of God's standard—is a sad truth (Romans 3:23). So why not be as merciful to others as you would like God to be to you? When you do, joy will follow!

*Thank You, Lord, for the blessings that come with being merciful to all!*

*https://biblehub.com/commentaries/matthew/5-7.htm

## PRAYER JAR INSPIRATION:

*I'm blessed in forgiving!*

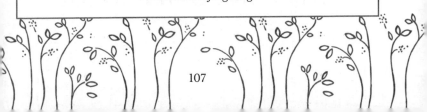

# THE CHALLENGE

*"You're familiar with the old written law, 'Love your
friend,' and its unwritten companion, 'Hate your enemy.'
I'm challenging that. I'm telling you to love your enemies.
Let them bring out the best in you, not the worst."*

MATTHEW 5:43-44 MSG

Sometimes, people can bring out the worst in us. But Jesus would like us to turn that around.

When someone treats you like an enemy, you're not to hate her. . .although that's how your flesh may first react. Instead, Jesus wants you to call on your better angels. To treat the offending party as a friend. To love her. To allow her to bring out the best in you, not the worst.

Perhaps your mother-in-law (or anyone else) makes comments about how you don't clean as well as she does, feed her son enough, or raise the kids right. Maybe it provokes anger in you. Before you know it, you start seeing red and treating her as if she were your enemy. But Jesus wants you to challenge that fleshly instinct. He wants you to let your spirit—the one that's aligned with His—overtake you. To respond to her in love, allowing whatever she says to bring out the best in you.

Are you up for that challenge?

*Allow Your love to overflow within me, Lord, so that even those who
act like my enemies will bring out the best—not the worst—in me.*

## PRAYER JAR INSPIRATION:

*May my enemies feel my love.*

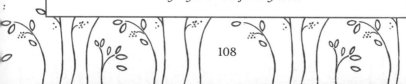

# UNLIMITED FORGIVENESS

*Then Peter came to him and asked, "Lord, how often should*
*I forgive someone who sins against me? Seven times?" "No,*
*not seven times," Jesus replied, "but seventy times seven!"*
MATTHEW 18:21-22 NLT

Some rabbis required their students to forgive only three times. So
when Peter asked Jesus if he should forgive seven times, he thought
he was being quite generous. But his self-satisfied balloon burst when
Jesus gave a much higher number: *seventy times* seven! Jesus was
making the point that when our offender is truly sorry, our forgiveness
should be unlimited.

Unlimited forgiveness sounds exhausting. But if there's no limit
with Jesus' forgiveness, there should be no limit to our own. Because
we are to be like Him in every way, we should abandon our attitudes
of revenge and malice toward those who hurt us. Instead, we're to
accept their apologies, treat them kindly, repay them with good, and
move on with our lives in love.

If you're having trouble meeting Jesus' unlimited forgiveness quota,
look to Him for the strength and the love you need. That's one prayer
He'll be sure to answer.

*Help me, Lord, to find a way to continually forgive*
*others as You continually forgive me.*

**PRAYER JAR INSPIRATION:**
*Praise God for His unlimited forgiveness!*

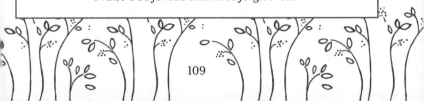

# SQUARING ACCOUNTS
# PARABLE: PART 1

*"The kingdom of God is like a king who decided to square accounts*
*with his servants. As he got under way, one servant was brought*
*before him who had run up a debt of a hundred thousand dollars.*
*He couldn't pay up, so the king ordered the man, along with his wife,*
*children, and goods, to be auctioned off at the slave market."*

MATTHEW 18:23-25 MSG

To help His followers understand more about forgiveness, Jesus told them a parable about a king who had a servant who couldn't pay his debt. So, the ruler decided he could recoup his money ($100,000) by having the man and his family sold off.

The servant begged the king for another chance to repay his debt. And in his compassion, the king erased his servant's debt.

That's what God has done for us. In fact, our debt to Him is so high, there's no way we could ever repay it. Thank God for His limitless mercy!

*Lord, Your mercy is forever and unfailing. For that I am truly grateful!*

## PRAYER JAR INSPIRATION:
*Praise the God of compassion!*

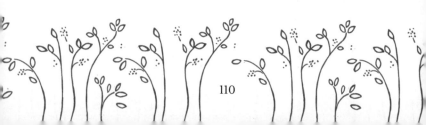

# SQUARING ACCOUNTS PARABLE: PART 2

*"His creditor wouldn't wait. He had the man arrested and put in prison until the debt could be paid in full. When some of the other servants saw this, they were very upset. They went to the king and told him everything that had happened."*

MATTHEW 18:30-31 NLT

Jesus' parable involved a king who had enough mercy and compassion to forgive the debt owed by a servant who had no way of paying him back. Yet, that same servant then refused to forgive a much smaller debt a fellow servant owed him! Instead of extending mercy, the first servant had the second thrown into prison until his debt could be paid. The king's other servants, hearing about this, ran to the king and let him know what was happening.

This is a reminder that we don't live in a vacuum. We serve a God who knows all and sees all. He is very much aware of what's being done to us. . .and how we're responding.

As women of the Way, we've been given the mandate to forgive repeatedly, just as God forgives us. And if we do not follow that mandate, we will reap the consequences.

Today, consider whom you might have "imprisoned" by not extending forgiveness. Then set that person—and yourself—free.

*Help me, Lord, to freely forgive my debtors, as You have forgiven me.*

## PRAYER JAR INSPIRATION:

*May I pay back forgiveness with forgiveness.*

# SQUARING ACCOUNTS
# PARABLE: PART 3

*In wrath his master turned him over to the torturers (the jailers), till he should pay all that he owed. So also My heavenly Father will deal with every one of you if you do not freely forgive your brother from your heart his offenses.*

MATTHEW 18:34-35 AMPC

"Freely forgive your brother from your heart his offenses." *From your heart* is the key here. We can grimace and "forgive" someone through gritted teeth, but that's not what God requires. He asks us to be sincere. To mean it when we say, "I forgive you." To stop continually replaying the wrong in our minds.

At the same time, we're not to be prideful about what we've done. We shouldn't announce with a dramatic sigh, "Yes, I forgave her. After all, that's what we're supposed to do," and then eat up all the compliments and reminders of how good we really are.

No. Our forgiveness isn't about getting a pat on the back. It's the God-mandated act of love we're to perform for each other as God does for us.

*Give me a heart for forgiveness, Lord,*
*for no other reason than to please You.*

# PRAYER JAR INSPIRATION:
*May I have God's love and His heart for forgiveness.*

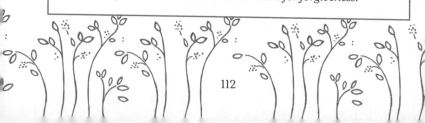

# FORGIVINGLY RESTORE

*Live creatively, friends. If someone falls into sin, forgivingly restore
him, saving your critical comments for yourself. You might be needing
forgiveness before the day's out. Stoop down and reach out to those
who are oppressed. Share their burdens, and so complete Christ's
law. If you think you are too good for that, you are badly deceived.*

GALATIANS 6:1-3 MSG

We are called by God to forgive others, just as they are called to
forgive us. So when someone slips up, it's not our role to give that
person a hard time about it. After all, we may someday find ourselves
in the same boat.

So, the next time you see someone err, fall into a snare, or simply
trip up, treat her with all the gentleness Christ demonstrated when
He walked this earth. Reach out, pick her back up, and help her stand
straight if needed. And spend some time with her, allowing her to
pour out her heart to you. In doing so, you will be loving her just as
Christ loves you.

*When people are hurting, Lord, help me to pick them up,
not add to their burdens. Give me the power and patience
to love and forgive, just as You love and forgive me.*

## PRAYER JAR INSPIRATION:

*May I offer an open ear, open arms, and an open heart
when my brother or sister needs forgiveness.*

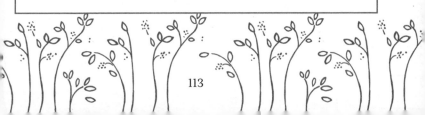

# LET IT GO

*And whenever you stand praying, if you have anything against anyone, forgive him and let it drop (leave it, let it go), in order that your Father Who is in heaven may also forgive you your [own] failings and shortcomings and let them drop.*

MARK 11:25 AMPC

In today's verse, Jesus tells His followers that if they want forgiveness from God, they must first forgive whoever has injured them, no matter how painful that injury was. And Jesus is not just asking them to forgive but to *let go* of whatever resentments still linger within their hearts.

If you're having difficulty with that, consider all the ways you've injured God with your own shortcomings—intentionally or unintentionally. And then think about all the times God has forgiven you. Remember back to the times when God could've thrown your prior misdeeds in your face but decided to forgive you instead. Then, pray that He would help you become more like His Son, who has already forgiven you and paid the price for your freedom to live in Him.

*Whenever I fold my hands to pray, Lord, help me to forgive others—to let go of any resentment I have toward them—so that You, in turn, will forgive me.*

---

## PRAYER JAR INSPIRATION:

*Jesus shows me not only how to forgive but how to let go. Thank You, Jesus!*

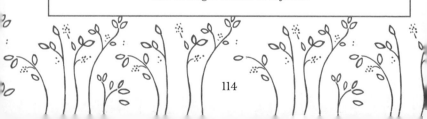

# SPIRITUAL LAW

*If you don't want to be judged, don't judge. If you don't want to be*
*condemned, don't condemn. If you want to be forgiven, forgive.*
*Don't hold back—give freely, and you'll have plenty poured back*
*into your lap—a good measure, pressed down, shaken together,*
*brimming over. You'll receive in the same measure you give.*

LUKE 6:37-38 VOICE

There is a spiritual law—one that often goes unrecognized in everyday life—that says whatever you do will come back around. If you judge others, you too will be judged. If you condemn others, you too will be condemned. And if you don't forgive others, you won't be forgiven either. Why? Because whatever you do (or don't do) will be done (or not done) to you. And it will be done (or not done) *to the same extent* that you do it (or don't do it).

So, today, think about how you are treating those who have transgressed against you or who owe you in some way. Taking this spiritual law into account, consider what you might need to do to make things right with them. Then, do it.

*Help me, Lord, to treat others as I would like*
*to be treated by them—and by You.*

## PRAYER JAR INSPIRATION:

*Lord, show me how to treat others the way You treat me!*

# STEPS TO FORGIVENESS

Has someone ever hurt you so badly that you didn't think you could forgive that person? Do you know God loves you so much that He wants you to experience a peace that passes understanding and the wonderful blessing of eternal life? We can't have that kind of peace if we don't forgive others.

Here are some basic steps to forgiving others: (1) Acknowledge the pain of being hurt. If we try to hide our emotions, it will cut us off from the process of forgiving others. (2) Spend some time thinking things through. Writing down what happened and putting it in your prayer jar or sharing your hurt with a trusted friend can be your second step toward forgiveness. (3) Think of a time when you asked for forgiveness. How did it make you feel? Did the person you'd wronged extend forgiveness or withhold it? God's Word instructs us to do to others what we would have them do to us (Matthew 7:12), so it can benefit us to put ourselves in someone else's shoes. (4) Remember God's willingness to forgive you. Since we have been forgiven, how can we hold on to grievances committed against us? (5) Let go of the hurt. Don't allow yourself to replay the offenses in your head. Let go of the pain and, with God's help, choose to move forward. (6) Pray for the person who hurt you (Matthew 5:44). Ask God to remove any negative emotions you may have.

# WHAT LIES BETWEEN

*See this pile of stones and this pillar which I have set between*
*us. This pile is a witness and this pillar is a witness that I will*
*not pass beyond this pile of stones to harm you, and you will*
*not pass beyond this pile and this pillar to harm me.*

GENESIS 31:51-52 VOICE

God gives us the strength to quickly move toward forgiving those who've wronged us. Yet, just because we must immediately *forgive* doesn't mean we must immediately *trust*.

Consider Laban and Jacob. Jacob, who'd deceived his brother Esau twice, ran for his life to Laban, his mother Rebekah's brother. There, Jacob fell in love with Laban's daughter Rachel. Jacob agreed to work seven years for Laban in exchange for Rachel as his wife. But on their wedding night, Laban delivered his oldest daughter Leah to the wedding tent! Later, he deceived Jacob again with some sheep.

When they finally parted, the two men realized they couldn't trust each other. So, although forgiveness was part of the arrangement, immediate trust was off the table.

Today, ask God for the strength to forgive. . .and for enough time for healing, and perhaps even renewed trust, to arrive.

*Lord, help me to heal amid forgiveness—*
*and perhaps eventually trust once more.*

## PRAYER JAR INSPIRATION:

*God helps me to immediately forgive and, when able, to forget.*

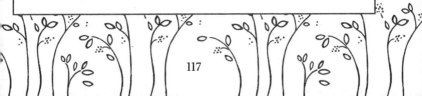

# NOTHING IS IMPOSSIBLE

*For with God nothing is ever impossible and no word from
God shall be without power or impossible of fulfillment.*

LUKE 1:37 AMPC

Sometimes, the harm others do to us seems irreparable. It feels impossible to forgive—much less forget. In these times, we must remember that everything is possible with God. That with His help and guidance, we should be able to accomplish whatever He commands us to do.

God has called us to forgive, so we must believe He will give us the power to do so. Perhaps that power will come from our prayers. Perhaps it will come from a greater understanding of Him and of the healing power in His Word. Perhaps it will come from a sermon or the wisdom found in a friend.

God will find a way to reach you, teach you, help you, heal you, and get you to a point where you can forgive and heal. All you need to do is open yourself to His help. . .and believe you will receive it.

*Help me, Lord, to forgive and heal. I open myself up to Your Word and
will, knowing You will respond and lead me where You want me to go.*

## PRAYER JAR INSPIRATION:

*Thank God that, with Him, nothing is impossible!*

# EVER-FLOWING FORGIVENESS

*"In prayer there is a connection between what God does
and what you do. You can't get forgiveness from God,
for instance, without also forgiving others. If you refuse to
do your part, you cut yourself off from God's part."*
MATTHEW 6:14-15 MSG

Imagine being cut off from God's ever-flowing forgiveness. That's what will happen if you refuse to forgive someone. Even if your pain is perfectly justified. Even if holding a grudge makes complete sense. No matter what, you are called to forgive. Because if you don't, you will cut yourself off from the lifeline of *God's* forgiveness.

It sounds harsh and a bit unfair, but in the spiritual world, it makes sense. It behooves you to understand that when you pray, a special link is formed between God's actions from heaven and your actions on earth. God will not answer your prayers for forgiveness until you also forgive others.

When you go to pray today, remember that you must do your part before asking God to do His. Otherwise, you will join ranks with the unforgiven.

*Lord, help me forgive others freely, just as You've done for me.*

## PRAYER JAR INSPIRATION:
*God will help me acquire ever-flowing forgiveness!*

# WELL OF PEACE VS.
# SPRING OF BITTERNESS

*Pursue peace with everyone, and holiness, since no one will see God without it. Watch carefully that no one falls short of God's favor, that no well of bitterness springs up to trouble you and throw many others off the path.*

HEBREWS 12:14-15 VOICE

God wants us to forgive others quickly and continually—to abide in a well of peace, not a spring of bitterness.

The quicker we are to forgive, the quicker peace is restored to us and those around us. Of course, there may be some bridges that need mending later. There may be some trust issues to work through. But the quicker we accept someone's apology (or offer our own), the quicker we will be at peace with ourselves, the other person, and God.

Consider the account of Jacob and Esau. After Jacob stole his brother Esau's birthright and blessing, the deceiver ran off to his mother's family and didn't see Esau again for twenty years! At that point, Jacob had no idea how angry his brother still was. And this tortured Jacob.

For the blessing of internal (and external) peace, find a way to forgive.

*Open my eyes and heart, Lord, to look within for signs of unrest.*
*Then, show me how to forgive so that I may walk the pathway of peace.*

## PRAYER JAR INSPIRATION:

*God, guide me to the well of peace.*

# GRUDGES VS. GOD

*Jacob: When you meet Esau . . .make sure you tell him,*
*"Your servant Jacob is coming along behind us."*
*(to himself) I might be able to appease Esau with these*
*gifts. He will see them before he sees me. When I see his*
*face, I'll know whether he'll accept and forgive me.*

GENESIS 32:19-20 VOICE

Although it was the hungry Esau who traded his birthright for a meal and later missed the opportunity to receive a blessing from his father, Isaac (Hebrews 12:16-17), his brother Jacob played a part in both situations. For Jacob was the one who offered his famished brother Esau a delicious meal (Genesis 25:27-34)—and later followed his mother's instructions by pretending to be Esau so that he could steal/receive their father's blessing (Genesis 27).

The point is, Jacob had angered his brother so much that Esau wanted to kill him. So, Jacob ran to his uncle Laban's house. Twenty years, four wives, and many children later, God told Jacob to head home (Genesis 31:3). When he received the report that Esau and four hundred of his men were coming to meet him, Jacob "was afraid and extremely distressed" (Genesis 32:7 VOICE)—even though God had promised to be with him (Genesis 31:3).

Remember, no matter who may hold grudges against you, God will be with you when you see them face-to-face.

*Lord, I thank You for Your presence, love, power, and promises.*

## PRAYER JAR INSPIRATION:
*God remains with me no matter what I may face.*

# PRAYERS AND PROMISES

*Then Jacob prayed. . . . Rescue me now, please, from the
hand of my brother, from the grip of Esau. I am afraid that
he may come and crush us all. . . . And Jacob prayed on.*

GENESIS 32:9, 11-12 VOICE

Riddled with fear that an angry Esau would destroy him and his family rather than receive his gifts, a restless and anxious Jacob did the only thing he could do: pray.

When we're up against the wall, unsure of how the future might play out and afraid that all our wrongs will come back to bite us, going to God in prayer is the best strategy.

Through humble prayer, we can review all the promises God has made on our behalf. We can remind ourselves that we are "not worthy of even a little of all of the loyal love and faithfulness You have shown to me, Your servant" (Genesis 32:10 VOICE). We can rehearse in our minds and hearts the fact that all our blessings have come from God and remain in Him, and that it is He alone who can rescue us from our fears and anxieties.

If fear is preventing you from asking for forgiveness, pray to God for peace of mind and heart.

*Lord, I humbly request courage and rescue as I
endeavor to seek another's forgiveness.*

## PRAYER JAR INSPIRATION:
*Through prayer, I'm assured of God's
promises, protection, and peace.*

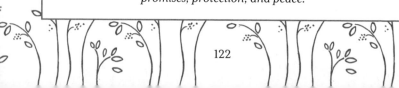

# TURNED HEARTS

*Jacob went on ahead. As he approached his brother,*
*he bowed to the ground seven times before him. Then*
*Esau ran to meet him and embraced him, threw his arms*
*around his neck, and kissed him. And they both wept.*

GENESIS 33:3-4 NLT

Going before his wives and children, Jacob approached his brother, bowing to the ground before him. And instead of suffering Esau's rage, Jacob received his love.

After a few minutes of introductions and conversation, Jacob explained that all his gifts were for Esau, "to ensure [his] friendship" (Genesis 33:8 NLT). And although Esau explained such gifts weren't necessary, Jacob insisted: "No, if I have found favor with you, please accept this gift from me. And what a relief to see your friendly smile. It is like seeing the face of God!" (Genesis 33:10 NLT). Because of Jacob's insistence, Esau finally accepted his brother's gifts.

Sometimes, we may be afraid to offer up an apology—especially if many years have passed since the damage was done. Yet, we should trust that God will produce a path for peace, no matter which side of the infraction we're on. He has a way of turning hearts around.

*I will always trust You, Lord, in the day of trouble. You alone have the power to make peace prevail. You alone can turn our hearts around.*

## PRAYER JAR INSPIRATION:

*My life and heart are in Your hands, Lord.*

123

# TRUST ISSUES

*"Well," Esau said, "let's be going. I will lead the way." But*
*Jacob replied. . . . "Please, my lord, go ahead of your servant.*
*We will follow slowly, at a pace that is comfortable for the*
*livestock and the children. I will meet you at Seir."*

GENESIS 33:12-14 NLT

Although Esau and Jacob warmly greeted each other, uncertainty still lingered in Jacob's mind. Perhaps in Esau's as well. Jacob wasn't very eager to follow right behind his brother. And when Esau offered to assign some of his own men to guide and protect him, Jacob responded, "That's not necessary. It's enough that you've received me warmly, my lord!" (Genesis 33:15 NLT).

When Esau turned and headed back to Seir, Jacob went on to Succoth then arrived at Shechem in Canaan, where he "set up camp outside the town" (Genesis 33:18 NLT). In other words, he settled away from his brother, never arriving at Seir.

Even when apologies have been offered and gifts have been presented, absolute reconciliation might never be attained. Trust may always be an issue. In such situations, once you've done all you can to offer your forgiveness and extend the olive branch of peace, it's best to leave the relationship in God's hands, willing to go where He leads.

*I look to You, Lord, for help in forgiving, forgetting,*
*and healing relationships. I go where You lead.*

## PRAYER JAR INSPIRATION:

*I move at God's pace, direction, and command.*

# THE JOY OF FORGIVENESS

*How happy is the one whose wrongs are forgiven, whose*
*sin is hidden from sight. How happy is the person whose*
*sin the Eternal will not take into account. How happy are*
*those who no longer lie, to themselves or others.*

PSALM 32:1-2 VOICE

One of the first steps to forgiveness is remembering that not only does God forgive your missteps, He removes them, pushing them away as far as the east is from the west (Psalm 103:12). When the Lord hears your prayers, you need not worry that He'll bring up your past blunders. He's wiped your slate clean as if you've never stepped out of line!

All of this forgiving and forgetting on God's part should be a source of pure joy to you! In fact, you should be running to the Lord, ready to confess whatever mistakes might stand between Him and you!

Today, when you pray and ask God to forgive you, do so with a humble, yet joyful, heart. Be grateful because you belong to the God who forgives and forgets.

*You make my heart sing, Lord! Thank You for*
*the blessings I find in Your forgiveness!*

## PRAYER JAR INSPIRATION:

*My Lord brings me joy because He forgives and forgets!*

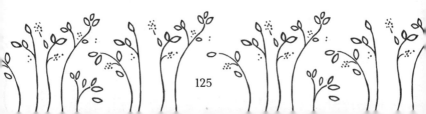

125

# ADMISSIONS

*When I refused to admit my wrongs, I was miserable, moaning
and complaining all day long so that even my bones felt brittle.
Day and night, Your hand kept pressing on me. My strength
dried up like water in the summer heat; You wore me down.*

PSALM 32:3-4 VOICE

Let's face it: when we mess up and try to hide our wrongs—or simply refuse to admit that we've erred—we begin to suffer. We become so miserable that we can barely breathe, so heavy is the sin that presses down upon us.

The Holy Spirit keeps reminding us of what we'd like to forget. But suppressing our misdeeds instead of confessing them wears us down emotionally, mentally, spiritually, and physically. John 16:8 tells us that the Holy Spirit convicts us of sin—and that God's forgiveness is the only remedy for the pain.

Today, do a wellness check on yourself. Ask the Spirit to bring to light any misdeeds that need God's remedy. And do so knowing His remedy always brings relief.

*Look me over, Spirit. See if there's anything within me that I
need to fess up to God. Then, after I've admitted all my wrongs
to God, fill me with the sweet relief found in Your forgiveness.*

## PRAYER JAR INSPIRATION:

*When I admit my wrongs, God assists with His relief!*

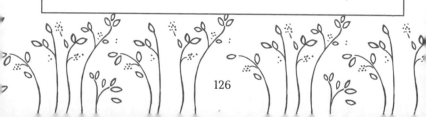

# CARRIED AWAY

*When I finally saw my own lies, I owned up to my sins*
*before You, and I did not try to hide my evil deeds from*
*You. I said to myself, "I'll admit all my sins to the Eternal,"*
*and You lifted and carried away the guilt of my sin.*

PSALM 32:5 VOICE

A child stands before you, her mouth smeared with chocolate cake. Icing decorates her cheeks and fingers. You ask, "Did you eat some of the cake I told you not to eat?" She shakes her head and says, "No, Mommy. I did *not* eat any cake."

*How ridiculous*, you think. Yet, many of us are just like that child. If we stood in front of a spiritual mirror, we'd see the lies and sins God sees. They're written all over our faces and pressing down upon our shoulders.

How much better for us to take a good look at ourselves and own up to our misdeeds. We can't hide them anyway—God sees all and *longs* to carry away our guilt.

Today, look in your spiritual mirror. Own up to God about whatever might be making you miserable. Expose all. And as soon as you do, He'll carry away your heavy burden of guilt.

*Thank You, Lord, for opening my eyes to all that weighs me down.*

## PRAYER JAR INSPIRATION:

*My God lifts and carries away my sin and guilt!*

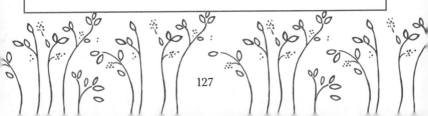

# THE HONESTY POLICY

*So let all who are devoted to You speak honestly to You now,*
*while You are still listening. For then when the floods come,*
*surely the rushing water will not even reach them.*

PSALM 32:6 VOICE

When we come to God with our hearts on our sleeves about our missteps—when we're honest and thorough in our confession—He not only cleanses us of guilt but gives us a sense of freedom, closure, and closeness. Having had a spirit-to-Spirit conversation with the Lord of all, we now feel one with Him again.

Then when the flood waters begin rising, we will stay far above them, unharmed because we are closely knit to our heavenly Father.

Honesty with the Lord is always the best policy. And the sooner, the better. Why wait to unburden yourself? Why not seek Him, fess up, and ask for His forgiveness when your heart is burdened with guilt?

Today, seek God's face, pour out your heart, and settle into His arms, comforted by His total forgiveness.

*Bend Your ear down to me, Lord, so that I can tell You all.*

---

## PRAYER JAR INSPIRATION:

*Following honest confessing, I find heavenly comfort and blessing.*

---

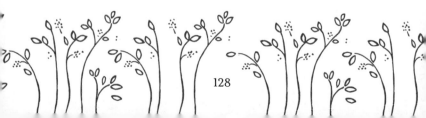

# HIDDEN IN GOD

*You are my hiding place. You will keep me out of trouble*
*and envelop me with songs that remind me I am free.*

PSALM 32:7 VOICE

When there is no concealing of sin (as if we can hide anything from God anyway), when there is no confession that needs to be made, when it's all square between you and your heavenly Father, He becomes your hiding place. Within the Lord, you are out of evil's reach. And instead of being mired in guilt, you are cocooned with songs that remind you of His freedom, grace, and love.

When you find yourself hidden in God—concealed in His Spirit, power, protection, and provision—you wonder why you ever tried to hide anything from Him to begin with. For there is such peace, light, and love when you are surrounded by His presence. In this wondrous abode, you are shielded from danger, kept from sin, and delighted by His mercy. You remember and revel in the joy and peace that drew you to the Lord in the first place.

And all you can do is linger in the comfort of His being, compelled to praise.

*Thank You, Lord, for Your shelter, mercy, protection, and love.*

## PRAYER JAR INSPIRATION:

*God is my hiding place, my refuge in the*
*storm, my cocoon of contentment.*

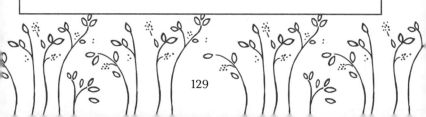

# OPEN AND EAGER

*I will teach you and tell you the way to go and how to get there;*
*I will give you good counsel, and I will watch over you.*

PSALM 32:8 VOICE

It's been a long journey, but you feel as if you have come home. The joy of God's forgiveness is fresh in your memory. You recall the time when you honestly admitted your errors to God and He, in turn, carried away and lifted the guilt of your sin. Instead of wanting to avoid Him, you've now made Him your hiding place.

Having been restored, you are open to God's instruction, eager to learn where to go next. And God has promised to teach you, to give you a roadmap so that you can walk away from temptation and lingering regrets. Here, in the safe and hidden refuge of God's presence, you can hear God whisper His words of wisdom in your ear. You can allow His grace to wash over you. You can revel in His promise to prevent you from ever falling in harm's way again.

Today, listen carefully to what God has to say.

*Speak, Lord, for my mind is open to Your direction.*
*My spirit is eager for Your wisdom.*

## PRAYER JAR INSPIRATION:
*God's wisdom directs my way. So, here I will stay and listen.*

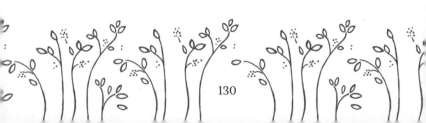

# YIELDING TO THE SPIRIT

*But don't be stubborn and stupid like horses and mules who, if not reined by leather and metal, will run wild, ignoring their masters.*

PSALM 32:9 VOICE

To stay in communion with God, you must be willing to listen to His voice, abide by His wisdom, and follow His counsel. So, the psalmist advises you not to act like a stubborn mule, braying and refusing to budge when God would have you be obedient.

Nor should you ignore God when He speaks. Instead, you are to keep both your eyes and ears open, eager to go where He leads. You must yield yourself—mind, body, soul, and spirit—to God. He won't force Himself on you; instead, He hopes you will see that His way is the only way to peace, love, comfort, and wisdom.

Are there areas in your life in which you've been running wild, bucking God's will? If so, it's time to yield your spirit to His, allowing His wisdom to gently lead your way.

*Help me, Lord, to be willing to listen, learn, and follow Your counsel.*

## PRAYER JAR INSPIRATION:
*I will yield myself to the Lord of life and love.*

# WRAPPED TIGHTLY

*Tormented and empty are wicked and destructive people, but the one*
*who trusts in the Eternal is wrapped tightly in His gracious love.*

PSALM 32:10 VOICE

When we abide by our own will—when we insist on our way rather
than God's or believe we needn't consult Him about every little
thing—we once more become tormented. Our lives become empty.
And soon enough, we find ourselves walking out of His will and onto
the road to destruction, annihilating all that gets in our way.

How much more wonderful life is when we give up the reins to
God, trusting that no matter how things appear, He knows what's best.

Trust God with all the big (and little) details of your life. Remember
that He has a grand plan—one that includes you! And soon, you will
find yourself in good company with the Lord of lords, embraced in
His loving arms, and placated by His peace and comfort.

*In You alone I trust, Lord. Thank You for giving*
*me a part in Your wondrous plan.*

## PRAYER JAR INSPIRATION:

*Trusting in God for all, I find myself cocooned in His gracious love.*

# JUMP FOR JOY

*Express your joy; be happy in Him, you who are good
and true. Go ahead, shout and rejoice aloud, you
whose hearts are honest and straightforward.*

PSALM 32:11 VOICE

Now that you've come clean with God, honestly admitted your missteps, realized the joy of His forgiveness, made Him your hiding place, opened yourself up to His will, and yielded yourself to Him in every way, go ahead and celebrate!

Revel in His company, wisdom, and protection. Live your guilt-free and heaven-blessed life with a smile on your face. Tell others what God has done in your life. You've shown guilt and stubbornness the door. Your heart is blessed and your spirit yielded. No more does guilt weigh you down or lies twist you in torment. You are hidden in the best refuge a woman could ask for—on this side of heaven! Your brow is free of worry; your heart is cleansed and strong.

Jump for joy!

*You've made me so happy, Lord! Thank You for giving peace
to my heart and joy to my spirit. You are my all in all!*

## PRAYER JAR INSPIRATION:

*Today, I will rejoice because I am happy in Him!*

# THE BLESSINGS CONTINUE

*[Eve] gave birth to another son and named him Seth.*
***Eve** (to herself): God has given me another child*
*to replace Abel, since Cain killed him.*
*After many years passed, Seth became the father of a son*
*and named him Enosh. This was about the time when people*
*began to worship and call on the name of the Eternal One.*

GENESIS 4:25-26 VOICE

Although Adam and Eve had sinned and been punished for their disobedience to God, He still loved them. He even promised them a Savior who would stomp out evil by stepping on Satan's head (Genesis 3:15).

And though Adam and Eve's relationship with God would never be the same, He continued to walk with them. Outside of the Garden of Eden, Adam and Eve produced their first child. How? Eve put it this way: "With the LORD's help, I have produced a man!" (Genesis 4:1 NLT). She named him Cain. She named her second child Abel.

After Eve lost Abel because he'd been murdered by Cain—and then lost Cain because he'd been banished by God—God continued to bless her by giving her another child named Seth.

Even when we err, God continues to forgive, provide, account for, and bless His children. With Him, blessings will continue to be found.

*Thank You, Lord, for all Your blessings!*

## PRAYER JAR INSPIRATION:

*All my blessings, including forgiveness,*
*continue to come from my God!*

# GRANTING
# FORGIVENESS

On October 2, 2006, a terrible incident occurred at West Nickel Mines in Pennsylvania. Charles Carl Roberts IV, a milk truck driver from a nearby town, entered a one-room Amish schoolhouse, shot ten young Amish girls, and then committed suicide.

The girls ranged from age six to thirteen. Three girls were killed immediately; two more died at local hospitals. Five additional girls were hospitalized with non-lethal injuries.

Many people from the Amish community—known for their religious devotion as well as for wearing traditional clothing and shunning certain modern conveniences—consoled Roberts' wife after the tragedy. Some of the Amish church members even attended his funeral. *How is that even possible?* you might wonder. It all stems from following God's command to forgive.

Although bad memories and deep wounds of the past can never be erased, they can be healed through the process of forgiveness. In the course of granting forgiveness, we receive the healing we desperately need.

# ADORNED IN LOVE

*Clothe yourselves with tenderhearted mercy, kindness, humility,*
*gentleness, and patience. Make allowance for each other's faults,*
*and forgive anyone who offends you. Remember, the Lord forgave*
*you, so you must forgive others. Above all, clothe yourselves*
*with love, which binds us all together in perfect harmony.*

COLOSSIANS 3:12-14 NLT

So many people are focused on taking care of their own and letting the rest of the world take care of itself. But Jesus asks you to adopt a different attitude—the one He wore. This attitude means clothing yourself with mercy, kindness, humility, gentleness, and patience. It means not only making allowances for each other's faults (for nobody is perfect) but forgiving anyone who offends you, just as you've been forgiven by God. Better yet, it means adorning yourself in love, allowing it to emanate from you, touching every person you meet!

Imagine what kind of a world we'd have if everyone shared all things, forgave, and loved each other. That is what you, through Christ's strength, are called to do today.

*Remind me each day, Lord, to clothe myself in*
*love—to forgive as You forgive me.*

## PRAYER JAR INSPIRATION:

*I dress myself today as Jesus dressed Himself—adorned with love!*

# FLAWED FORGIVERS

*Jesus is not some high priest who has no sympathy for our*
*weaknesses and flaws. He has already been tested in every way that*
*we are tested; but He emerged victorious, without failing God.*

HEBREWS 4:15 VOICE

Just as Jesus has sympathy for us—knowing our weakness and our flaws and making allowance for both—so must we have sympathy for others. For unlike Jesus, we are not perfect.

Yes, believe it or not, we are flawed females. It's only through Jesus and His power and love that we can get closer to perfection. That means not worrying so much about our outside but focusing instead on what is happening on the inside.

Today, think about someone who has recently tested or offended you. Then, tap into the power of Jesus. Remember all the times He was insulted, whipped, kicked, and mocked—robbed of His clothes as well as His dignity. Consider how He lingered on the cross, His beloved family and followers watching and unable to help.

If Jesus can forgive all that was done to Him, surely you can forgive what's done to you.

*Help me, Lord, to forgive as You forgave. Help me*
*tap into Your power and emerge victorious!*

## PRAYER JAR INSPIRATION:
*Jesus inspires the imperfect me to forgive imperfect others.*

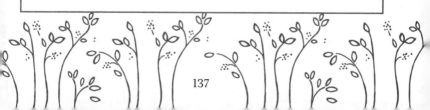

# A REFLECTION OF JESUS

*"Let me give you a new command: Love one another. In the same way I loved you, you love one another. This is how everyone will recognize that you are my disciples—when they see the love you have for each other."*

JOHN 13:34-35 MSG

We are called to be like Jesus. That means we need to love like Him.

One way to look very much *un*like Jesus is to hold grudges and take revenge on those who've done you wrong. Or to leap with joy when the person who has injured you gets injured himself—to say in your mind, *Well, he got his just desserts.*

Consider your behavior as a Christian woman. How might others view Jesus knowing you are one of His followers? Will they see Him as the embodiment of love, peace, kindness, and compassion? Or will they see Him as hateful and bent on revenge?

*I want to be like You, Jesus. Help me love as You loved.*
*Help me lean into You, to forgive as You forgave.*

## PRAYER JAR INSPIRATION:

*With God's power, I will endeavor to love as Jesus loved.*

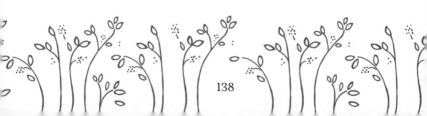

# WHOLLY FORGIVE

*He was hurt because of us; he suffered so. Our wrongdoing*
*wounded and crushed him. He endured the breaking that made*
*us whole. The injuries he suffered became our healing.*

ISAIAH 53:5 VOICE

It was our misdeeds that brought Jesus willingly to His knees. Our
sins were the thorns embedded in His head, the nails piercing His
hands and feet, the spear jabbed into His side. And He bore all that
for us before we even knew Him—before we were even born! Why?
Because He loved us like no one ever has or will.

Jesus did all this so that we would find God and be reconciled to
Him through His forgiveness. His sufferings became our ultimate
healing. Through Him, we receive God's grace, mercy, and forgiveness,
and we are brought back to life.

When we understand and focus on what Jesus did for us, surely
we can overlook our own injuries and grievances and seek a way to
forgive. Doing so will bring satisfaction to the One who suffered so
much for us!

*Jesus, help me seek a path to forgiveness. My suffering*
*is nothing compared to Yours for me.*

## PRAYER JAR INSPIRATION:

*Because of Jesus' suffering, I can find a way to wholly forgive.*

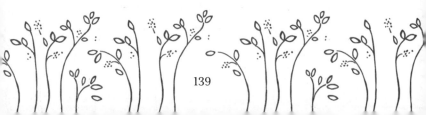

# PASSING IT ON

*All praise goes to God, Father of our Lord Jesus, the Anointed One.*
*He is the Father of compassion, the God of all comfort. He consoles*
*us as we endure the pain and hardship of life so that we may draw*
*from His comfort and share it with others in their own struggles.*

2 Corinthians 1:3-4 voice

In every calamity we suffer—every trouble that trips us up—we receive God's comfort, compassion, and consolation. As soon as He sees a tear fall from our eyes or hears the deep sigh of a heavy heart, He rushes to our side and offers all the love and comfort we need. And He does this so that we can offer the same mercy, comfort, and compassion to others.

When others bring us heartache, God sends His comfort. So, why not offer the comfort of our forgiveness and mercy to the ones who wound us? Why not extend what God has extended to us?

The next time you experience God's compassion, pass it on to one who may not expect yours. Take in the comfort you've received from heaven and give it to someone else.

*Thank You, Lord, for being a source of comfort when I'm*
*wounded. Help me pass that comfort on by not only forgiving*
*my offenders but loving them and lifting their pain.*

## PRAYER JAR INSPIRATION:

*The compassion and comfort God gives to me*
*are what I aim to pass on to others.*

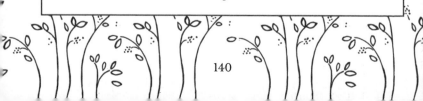

# GOING THAT EXTRA MILE

*As for the one who wants to sue you and take away
your shirt, let him have your coat as well. And if anyone
forces you to go one mile, go with him two.*

MATTHEW 5:40-41 HCSB

One of the first words children say is "Mine!" This usually happens when other kids take their favorite toy, treating it like their own. Then, when we grow older and see a sister wearing our favorite shirt, we say a longer sentence—something like, "Did you get that out of my closet? That's mine! Take it off right now!" Sounds childish, right?

Yet, such possessiveness can continue into adulthood. Many families are torn apart when their parents leave this mortal coil and the children begin arguing over what part of the estate they believe is rightfully theirs.

God wants us to have a selfless servant's heart, not a selfish child's. So, when something you believe is rightfully yours is taken, forgive the taker. And then go a step further and give the taker even *more*. When you go that extra mile, you may be pleasantly surprised by the extra blessing you receive.

*Lord, give me a servant's heart that's full of forgiveness and selflessness.*

## PRAYER JAR INSPIRATION:

*With a servant's heart, I am doubly blessed.*

# A SIMPLE RULE OF THUMB

*"Here is a simple rule of thumb for behavior: Ask yourself what you want people to do for you; then grab the initiative and do it for them! If you only love the lovable, do you expect a pat on the back? Run-of-the-mill sinners do that. If you only help those who help you, do you expect a medal? Garden-variety sinners do that. If you only give for what you hope to get out of it, do you think that's charity? The stingiest of pawnbrokers does that."*

LUKE 6:31-34 MSG

You aren't just some common female. You're a woman of God. And as such, you're to follow a simple rule of thumb: "Think of the kindness you wish others would show you; do the same for them" (Luke 6:31 VOICE). That means living with a heart of compassion, a spirit of kindness, and a soul filled with forgiveness.

Have you ever done something that seemed unforgivable? How did you feel when you were forgiven? When you weren't? How much would your life have changed if you had been?

The point is that sometimes, people won't deserve your forgiveness. . .but you should do it anyway. Why? Because You're a woman of the Way. And that's what we do!

*Lord, help me love the unlovable and forgive the unforgivable.*

---

## PRAYER JAR INSPIRATION:

*With God's help, may I do for others what I would have them do for me!*

# TURN AND CHOOSE

*I gave you the choice today between life and death, between
being blessed or being cursed. Choose life, so that you and your
descendants may live! If you love the Eternal your God and listen to
His voice and always remain loyal to Him, for He is your life, then
you'll be able to live a long time in the land the Eternal promised.*

DEUTERONOMY 30:19-20 VOICE

In Deuteronomy 28:1-14, Moses, speaking for God, lists all the
blessings—including life—that God-followers will receive if they
love and obey Him. But in Deuteronomy 28:15-68, Moses lists all the
curses—including death—if the same people *don't* love and obey God.

Jesus calls His followers to forgive others. Yet, this isn't something
you can do in your own power. Instead, you must remind yourself to
"turn to the Lord your God with all your [mind and] heart and with
all your being" (Deuteronomy 30:10 AMPC).

If you find yourself in a situation where it's very difficult to pardon
someone who has wronged you, remember that God's forgiving power
is available to you. Simply turn to Him with your entire being. Tell
Him where your difficulty lies. Then, ask Him to overflow you with
His love, forgiveness, power, and provision, knowing that this is where
your life and blessings lie.

*Help me, Lord. Fill me with Your power to forgive.*

## PRAYER JAR INSPIRATION:

*With God's help, I can find a way to forgive all.*

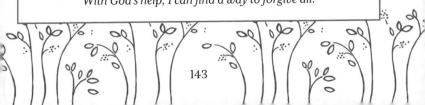

# FORGIVING THE FORGIVER

*I am a woman of a sorrowful spirit. . . . I was pouring out*
*my soul before the Lord. . . . Out of my great complaint*
*and bitter provocation I have been speaking.*

1 SAMUEL 1:15-16 AMPC

There may come a time when you have some difficulty forgiving God Himself—for prayers that weren't answered the way you expected, for the tragic death of a loved one, for failed plans you thought God was backing, for not being able to rein in the world's cruelty, for a miracle that never came, for the evil giant who won over you, etc.

When a believer is unable to "forgive God" for what she's suffered, chances are good that she'll leave the church or, even worse, badmouth God to believers and nonbelievers alike! Why? Because she is riddled with disappointment in the Almighty Himself.

The Bible is filled with examples of people who were disappointed and angry with God—including David, the apple of God's eye (2 Samuel 6:1-8); Jonah (3:10-4:1-4); Jeremiah (15:18); and Moses (Numbers 11:10-15).

Fortunately, God understands. He knows our emotions can wreak havoc on our thoughts. During these times, we need to vent our feelings, pour out our hearts, and ask God to help us restore our relationship with Him.

*Lord, I offer my heart, sore and heavy.*

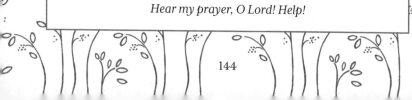

## PRAYER JAR INSPIRATION:
*Hear my prayer, O Lord! Help!*

# WISDOM PLEASE!

*If you are wise and understand God's ways, prove it by living an honorable life, doing good works with the humility that comes from wisdom. . . . The wisdom from above is first of all pure. It is also peace loving, gentle at all times, and willing to yield to others. It is full of mercy and the fruit of good deeds. It shows no favoritism and is always sincere.*

JAMES 3:13, 17 NLT

Our fellow humans would have us seek revenge against those who've wronged us—to repay evil for evil. God has a better, more peaceable way.

When you need to forgive the unforgivable but don't know how, ask God for both His power and His wisdom. His wisdom, after all, is far above anyone else's.

When you ask God for wisdom, He will give you all the love and gentleness you need to forgive others. He will change your mindset from revenge to restoration, from payback to peace, from maliciousness to mercy, from victim to victor.

*Lord, I don't know the first steps toward forgiving the person who wronged me. So I'm coming to You for help, power, and wisdom so that I can repay this stroke of evil with good.*

## PRAYER JAR INSPIRATION:

*God's wisdom is my salvation.*

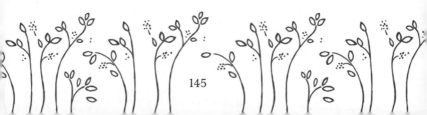

# NO HATRED OR HARPING

*Hatred starts fights, but love pulls a quilt over the bickering. . . .*
*He who covers and forgives an offense seeks love, but he who*
*repeats or harps on a matter separates even close friends.*

PROVERBS 10:12 MSG; 17:9 AMPC

When it comes to forgiving and forgetting, you can take either the path of hatred and harping or the path of love.

Hatred will stir up whatever past grievances you've suffered. Every time the "forgiven" individual slights you, past wounds suddenly spring open. Suspicions and doubts crop up, turning every small offence into a major one. Harping over the past prevents wounds from healing in the present.

Rather than spend your time hating and harping—continually rehearsing how you've been injured—turn to your friend with love. Let go of whatever has been holding you back from forgiveness.

If you need help bearing such a situation, go to God. Ask Him for a calm spirit, a willing heart, and all the love you need to mend a fractured relationship.

*Lord, help me walk the path of love, letting bygones*
*be bygones. For You Yourself are love.*

## PRAYER JAR INSPIRATION:
*The Lord of love will help me lead with love.*

# GOD'S DREAMS PREVAIL

*This time he told the dream to his father as well as to his brothers,*
*but his father scolded him. "What kind of dream is that?"*
*he asked. "Will your mother and I and your brothers actually come*
*and bow to the ground before you?" But while his brothers were*
*jealous of Joseph, his father wondered what the dreams meant.*

GENESIS 37:10-11 NLT

Through dreams, God had informed Joseph that he would one day be in a position of superiority over his family. But his brothers didn't take the information well. Who was this stripling to think he would one day rule over his elders? The only one who later remembered Joseph's dream was Israel, his father.

Soon after Joseph told others of his dreams, his older brothers committed misdeeds to put the younger in his place. Yet in doing so, they became a means to the end Joseph had envisioned.

You, too, may have had dreams that others have scorned or tried to thwart. God wants you to forgive them and move on, knowing that His dreams for your life—His visions for your future—will prevail against the actions of others.

*Help me, Lord, to keep my eyes on Your vision for my future*
*and to forgive those who try to thwart my progress.*

## PRAYER JAR INSPIRATION:
*Humans may scheme, but God's dreams for me will prevail.*

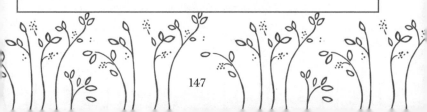

# WHEN YOU'RE IN THE PITS

*Joseph's Brothers (to each other): Oh, here comes the great dreamer. Let's kill him and throw his body into one of the pits. Then we can tell everyone a wild animal killed and devoured him. We'll see then what becomes of his stupid dreams.*

GENESIS 37:19-20 VOICE

Joseph's brothers' jealousy of his place in their father's heart, as well as their suspicion that his dreams might indeed come true, caused them to act against their brother. They plotted to kill Joseph—their own sibling—in cold blood! Talk about a rift in the family!

Yet Reuben, the eldest son of Israel, stepped in and kept his brothers from slaying Joseph. They put him in a pit instead (from which Rueben hoped to later rescue him). Then, when Rueben wasn't looking, the brothers decided to sell Joseph to some traders.

There may be times when you feel as if everything is out of your control. When others, looking out for their own interests, are taking advantage of you and scheming to use your misfortune for their benefit. When this happens, learn to forgive them, remembering God will always work things out for good for His children.

*Help me keep looking for the light of Your plan when I'm in the pits, Lord. Help me forgive what seems unforgivable, knowing You have a good plan for us all.*

## PRAYER JAR INSPIRATION:
*The Lord shines His light in my darkness.*

# FORGIVING IN ABSENTIA

*When Potiphar heard his wife's account, his face flushed with anger.*
*So Potiphar, Joseph's master, put him into prison and locked him*
*up in the place where the king's prisoners were confined. Joseph*
*remained there for a time. But the Eternal One remained with Joseph.*

GENESIS 39:19-21 VOICE

Joseph was taken to Egypt and sold to Potiphar, an officer of Pharoah. Seeing that God was with Joseph and made all that he did succeed, Potiphar put Joseph in charge of his entire household.

Every day, Potiphar's wife, who was attracted to Joseph, tried to get him to sleep with her. But the boy refused. One day, when no one else was around, Potiphar's wife grabbed Joseph by his clothes in an attempt to seduce him. But Joseph ran away. So, she cried rape—not only to her servants but also to her husband. . .and her false accusation landed Joseph in prison. Yet, no matter what happened in his life, Joseph stuck to God, and God stuck to him.

Joseph may have never again laid eyes on Potiphar's wife. But chances are, because he was right with God, he forgave her in absentia. He let go and let God—a good rule of thumb for all followers of the right Way.

*Help me, Lord, to always walk Your way—to let go of my*
*pain through forgiveness and to let You lead me on.*

## PRAYER JAR INSPIRATION:
*Every day, I will let go of grudges and let God lead me on the Way.*

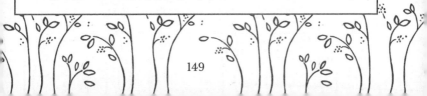

# FORGIVING AND FORGOTTEN

*The chief jailor, like Potiphar, didn't need to worry about anything that was in Joseph's care because the Eternal One was with him. And whatever Joseph did worked out well because the Eternal made it so.*

GENESIS 39:23 VOICE

From the pit to Potiphar to prison, Joseph continued believing in God, holding to the tenets of his faith. In return, God continued to bless the boy, trial after trial.

While in prison, Joseph, with God's help, interpreted the dreams of some of Pharoah's servants. The royal baker, he predicted, would be killed, while the royal cupbearer would live to serve the Egyptian king once more. Joseph then asked the cupbearer to remember him, to mention him to Pharoah when his life grew brighter. Maybe the king would free him from the dungeon.

But for a time, Joseph remained forgotten.

Has someone whom you've helped ever injured you by forgetting about you? If you're still holding on to that grudge, let it go. Know that God will continue to work in your life regardless of others' actions. . .or inactions. Perhaps one day, the one you forgave will remember you (Genesis 41:9).

*Help me be one who forgives those who have forgotten me, Lord. For I know that when I walk in Your will, You will always find a way for me.*

## PRAYER JAR INSPIRATION:
*I will forgive those who forget, knowing God will always remember me [Isaiah 49:15-16].*

# CLOSE TO GOD

*Pharaoh said to Joseph, . . ."I have heard that when you hear about a dream you can interpret it." "It is beyond my power to do this," Joseph replied. "But God can tell you what it means and set you at ease."*

GENESIS 41:15-16 NLT

Up to this point, Joseph been wronged by a lot of people. It began with his brothers stripping him of the special coat his father had given him, putting him in a pit, and selling him to traders. It continued as he was a slave in Potiphar's house, where Potiphar's wife unjustly accused Joseph of rape. And it persisted in prison, when Joseph correctly interpreted the dreams of two of Pharaoh's servants, only to be forgotten for *two years* by the one who lived.

But through all Joseph's hardships, trials, and seemingly bad breaks, he remained so close to God that he gave God the credit for all he did.

When you remain so close to God that you forget where you begin and He ends, forgiveness becomes natural. When you're certain God is working His good plan in your life, hardships don't seem quite as hard.

*Lord, pull me close. Help me rest in the certainty that You're working Your plan through my life.*

## PRAYER JAR INSPIRATION:

*God, draw me into Your presence.*

# FRUITFUL AMID MISFORTUNE

*Pharaoh (to his advisors): Is there anyone else you know like Joseph who has the Spirit of God within him?*
*(to Joseph) Since God has shown all of this to you, I can't imagine anyone wiser and more discerning than you.*

GENESIS 41:38-39 VOICE

Joseph was seventeen years old when his brothers threw him into a pit. For the next thirteen years, he would be a slave or a prisoner. Yet, not once did he curse his brothers or Potiphar's wife or the king's servants. Instead, he stuck with God. And by holding on to God and the dream God had given him, Joseph became so wise that he ended up as Pharoah's right-hand man!

This dreamer of dreams allowed God to speak through him so that Pharoah would understand the meaning of his own dreams. There would be seven years of plenty, during which Joseph would store much grain. That way, when the famine came, the people wouldn't starve.

When you stick with God, you'll find Him helping you forgive the wrongs done against you, forget all your hardships, and become fruitful amid misfortune (Genesis 41:51-52).

*Lord, thank You for helping me forget my hardships, forgive those who've done me wrong, and follow You in this path of life.*

## PRAYER JAR INSPIRATION:

*With God's help, my forgiving and forgetting the misdeeds of others will keep me fruitful amid misfortune.*

# THE TESTING

*If you really are honest men, choose one of your brothers to remain in prison. The rest of you may go home with grain for your starving families. But you must bring your youngest brother back to me.*

GENESIS 42:19-20 NLT

Needing to feed their starving families, Joseph's brothers came to Egypt to get some grain. Although it had been twenty years since he'd seen them, Joseph recognized them at once. . .yet they didn't recognize him. As the brothers bowed before Joseph, he remembered the dreams God had planted in his mind all those years ago.

Joseph, speaking to them quite gruffly, accused them of being spies. Then, having heard their story, he put them in prison and told them one would be sent home to fetch the youngest brother. Then, he decided to keep Simeon in prison while the brothers took the grain to their families. They were to then return with the youngest brother in tow.

Joseph had long-ago forgiven his brothers, but he wasn't yet ready to trust how they'd behave toward him. He needed to be sure they'd repented before he let them back into his life.

Although He forgives, God also tests our hearts sometimes, seeking our repentance for our misdeeds. Once proven, we'll hopefully come out like gold.

*Lord, thank You for helping me forgive others.*
*Now help me to find a way to trust again.*

## PRAYER JAR INSPIRATION:

*God, give me the wisdom to know when to*
*trust again—and the strength to do it.*

# TENDER HEARTS

*Speaking among themselves, they said, "Clearly we are*
*being punished because of what we did to Joseph long ago.*
*We saw his anguish when he pleaded for his life, but we*
*wouldn't listen. That's why we're in this trouble."*

GENESIS 42:21 NLT

The brothers had heard Joseph's proposal: First, they were to choose a brother to stay in prison in Egypt while they took the grain back to their families. Then, they were to return with their youngest brother (Benjamin), thus proving to Joseph that they were telling the truth.

They began to talk among themselves, not realizing this high Egyptian official (a.k.a. Joseph) could understand every word they were saying. The entire time, they'd been communicating with him through an interpreter.

Overhearing his brothers' conversation, Joseph discovered that the eldest, Reuben, had stood against his brothers' treachery toward Joseph many years ago. Tears sprung up in Joseph's eyes, forcing him to turn away. Then, when he'd composed himself, he had Simeon tied up and sent the brothers on their way.

When we do wrong and begin to repent, think of the tears that must spring up in the eyes of God Himself. Perhaps knowing this will help us forgive those who have wronged us.

*Lord, give me a heart for forgiveness, one as tender as Yours.*

## PRAYER JAR INSPIRATION:

*May I tenderly forgive others as God tenderly forgives me.*

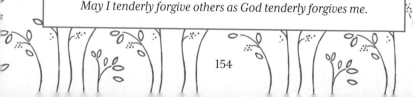

# SCENARIO OF SEPARATION

*The waiters served Joseph at his own table, and his brothers were served at a separate table. The Egyptians who ate with Joseph sat at their own table, because Egyptians despise Hebrews and refuse to eat with them. Joseph told each of his brothers where to sit, and to their amazement, he seated them according to age, from oldest to youngest.*

GENESIS 43:32-33 NLT

Having run out of food for their father and their families, Joseph's brothers went back to Egypt for more. But this time, they returned not only with the money that'd been left in their first sacks of grain but with their youngest brother Benjamin in tow, thus meeting Joseph's stipulation. They were also reunited with their brother Simeon, whom Joseph had kept in Egypt until the brothers returned with the younger.

Now they were seated at feast tables. . .but Joseph sat at a table alone.

This scenario is not unlike the separation our unconfessed sins cause between us and our Master. Yet, just as soon as we admit our wrongdoings and repent, the sluice gates of love, joy, and forgiveness are opened.

What unconfessed sin or attitude of unforgiveness might be preying on your own mind, separating you from your Master?

*Lord, there's something I've been meaning to tell You. . . .*

## PRAYER JAR INSPIRATION:
*May nothing separate me from Thee, Lord.*

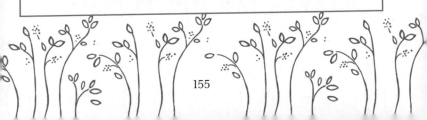

# STARTLING REVELATIONS

*I am your brother, Joseph, whom you sold into Egypt. Don't be upset or angry with yourselves any longer because of what you did. You see God sent me here ahead of you to preserve life.*

GENESIS 45:4-5 VOICE

Joseph could hold out no longer. He sent all from the room except his brothers. Heaven knows how hard the brothers' hearts must've been pounding at this point!

Alone at last with his siblings, this high Egyptian official began to weep. . .and then he revealed his true identity.

His brothers were so shocked they couldn't speak. When he asked them to come closer, they did so cautiously. For before them stood their little brother, the dreamer they'd envied so long ago. It was their anger that had prompted them to throw him into a pit and later sell him to traders. But now, the youth they'd brought to anguish was the ruler of a great empire—upon which their very lives now depended!

Like Joseph, Jesus reaches out to you, longing for you to come close and understand the depths of His compassion and loving-kindness. And once you've returned to Him and repented of your misdeeds, He longs to comfort you.

Come closer. Run into His loving arms.

*Jesus, thank You for reaching out to me, looking to comfort and love me when I return to Your presence.*

## PRAYER JAR INSPIRATION:

*Jesus loves me, this I know!*

# SOMETHING GOOD

*God sent me here ahead of you to make sure you and your
families survive this terrible ordeal and have a remnant left on
earth. So it wasn't really you who sent me here, but God;
the same God who made me an advisor to Pharaoh, master of
his household, and ruler over everyone in the land of Egypt.*

GENESIS 45:7-8 VOICE

Joseph's brothers had fallen in their walk with God. They had brought
trouble and grief to their dreaming brother. Yet, the Lord used their
mistakes to bring about something good. And Joseph realized that.
He reframed his brothers' misdeeds as part of God's plan to ensure
the survival and well-being of His children!

This does not mean the brothers' *sins* were good; it means that
out of that evil, God *made* something good. And in this, Joseph and
his brothers rejoiced—they were once more reconciled to each other.

Imagine if we all would reframe others' misdeeds in our minds
instead of holding a grudge! To just believe God will turn even the
sourest of sins into something good!

*Help me, Lord, to always remember that no matter what maladies
or misfortunes befall me, You will make something good out of it!*

## PRAYER JAR INSPIRATION:
*God will work all things out for my good.*

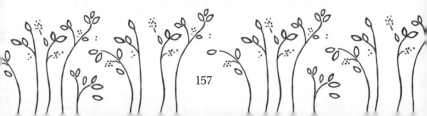

# FULLY FORGIVEN

*When Joseph's brothers began to realize the implications of
their father's death, Joseph's brothers began to worry.*
**Joseph's Brothers:** *What if Joseph still bears a grudge
in some way against us and decides to pay us back
in full for all of the wrong we did to him?*

GENESIS 50:15 VOICE

After Joseph had revealed himself to his brothers, he sent them back
to their father, telling them to journey from the drought-stricken
land of Canaan to Egypt, where he would take care of them and their
families. And so they did, settling in the land of Goshen, where the
130-year-old Jacob (a.k.a. Israel) lived his remaining years.

After their father's death at age 147, the brothers, no longer pro-
tected beneath their father's shadow, began to worry that Joseph still
held a grudge against them. Perhaps now he would exact his revenge.
So, they sent Joseph a message, humbling themselves and telling him
that their father had begged him to forgive his brothers' crimes.

No sin is worth the guilty conscience that's gained upon committing
it. As the brothers humbled themselves before Joseph, so should we
humble ourselves before God, pleading for His reassurance that we
are indeed fully forgiven.

*Lord, help me let go of the guilt for the sin from which You
pardoned me. Help me realize that in You, I am fully forgiven.*

## PRAYER JAR INSPIRATION:

*Jesus, upon Your forgiveness, I pray You
would wipe my conscience clean!*

# NO-JUDGMENT ZONE

*Joseph: Don't be afraid. Am I to judge instead of God? It is not my place. Even though you intended to harm me, God intended it only for good, and through me, He preserved the lives of countless people, as He is still doing today. So don't worry.*

GENESIS 50:19-21 VOICE

When we hold on to grudges, we find ourselves blocking God's work—work that will repair any damage done and will produce blessings in and through our lives. That's the point Joseph made to his brothers.

God alone is judge over our deeds. It's not a follower's place to decide what punishment others should receive. Instead, we are to allow any ill will we have against others to dissolve in our mind, hearts, spirits, souls, and speech. Give it up to God. Then ask Him to bring good from the evil, knowing He specializes in this impossible task. You must only offer yourself up as a conduit to whatever grace God wants to extend to you and to others.

*I'm thankful, God, that I'm not the one responsible for judging the actions of others. All I must do is allow You to work Your will through me, knowing You intend to make all evil into something good!*

## PRAYER JAR INSPIRATION:

*Here I am, Lord. Use me as You see fit!*

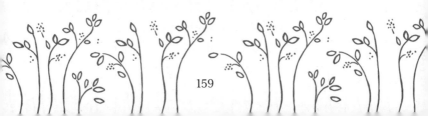

# BITTER LOSS

*Call me not Naomi [pleasant]; call me Mara [bitter], for the Almighty has dealt very bitterly with me. I went out full, but the Lord has brought me home again empty. Why call me Naomi, since the Lord has testified against me, and the Almighty has afflicted me?*

RUTH 1:20-21 AMPC

During the days when Israel lived under judges, there was a famine in Judah. Rather than staying where God wanted them, a man named Elimelech, his wife Naomi, and their sons Mahlon and Chillion headed to the greener pastures of Moab. There, Naomi's husband and her sons, who'd wed Moabitesses, died, leaving her and her daughters-in-law as widows.

Yet, Naomi didn't go to God and ask His forgiveness; instead, she blamed Him for her plight. She returned home with nothing and no one—except her daughter-in-law Ruth. There, Naomi asked to be called *Mara*, which means "bitterness."

God's Word clearly teaches we mustn't allow a root of bitterness to grow within us. When afflicted, we should turn to God with humble hearts, ask His forgiveness, and bear our troubles with a hopeful heart, knowing He will make something good from our missteps.

*Lord, forgive me for walking out of Your will. Help me bear up under my trouble, knowing You will make something good come from my disobedience.*

## PRAYER JAR INSPIRATION:

*Help me let go of my bitterness, Lord, and hang on to the hope I find in You.*

# FROM FAITH TO BLESSING

*"I also know about everything you have done for your mother-in-law since the death of your husband. I have heard how you left your father and mother and your own land to live here among complete strangers. May the Lord, the God of Israel, under whose wings you have come to take refuge, reward you fully for what you have done."*

RUTH 2:11-12 NLT

Ruth had seen some hard times too. She'd witnessed the death of her father-in-law, brother-in-law, and husband. Yet, she refused to abandon her mother-in-law, Naomi (a.k.a. Mara). And unlike her mother-in-law, Ruth took action.

Ruth had already confessed that she wanted to follow not just Naomi but her God. "Where you go I will go," she'd said, "and where you lodge I will lodge. Your people shall be my people and your God my God. Where you die I will die, and there will I be buried. The Lord do so to me, and more also, if anything but death parts me from you" (Ruth 1:16-17 AMPC). And when she arrived in Bethlehem, she worked to support both herself and Naomi.

Ruth didn't hold a grudge against God but instead sought His presence, seeing Him as her refuge.

*May I live my life without bitterness, Lord, knowing that my blessing lies in my willingness to faithfully seek You as my Refuge.*

## PRAYER JAR INSPIRATION:

*God is my gain and my port of Refuge.*

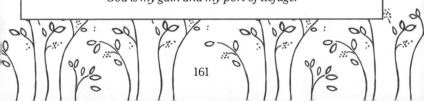

# THE DEEPEST NEED MET

*Some men came carrying a paralyzed man on a sleeping mat.*
*They tried to take him inside to Jesus, but they couldn't reach*
*him because of the crowd. So they went up to the roof and*
*took off some tiles. Then they lowered the sick man on his mat*
*down into the crowd, right in front of Jesus. Seeing their faith,*
*Jesus said to the man, "Young man, your sins are forgiven."*

Luke 5:18-20 nlt

The account in Luke 5:17-26 begins with Jesus teaching in a house when "the Lord's healing power was strongly with Jesus" (Luke 5:17 nlt). Some men, unable to get their friend close to Jesus because of the crowd, lowered him through an opening they made in the roof.

Immediately, just by looking at the invalid, Jesus could see that the man's deepest and most urgent need was forgiveness. Why else would He have offered it before all other remedies?

We are like this man. Our deepest need—and our best gift—is Jesus' forgiveness. For only after we've applied for and received His pardon are our worries and anxieties chased away. This is our biggest miracle—forgiveness from the perfect Son of God. No amount of wealth or fame can give us the freedom, clarity, and peace of Jesus' pardon.

*Lord, please bring to my mind anything for which I*
*need forgiveness. Then, grant me that gift.*

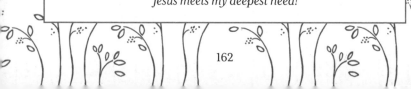

# PRAYER JAR INSPIRATION:

*Jesus meets my deepest need!*

# ADDING YOUR BELIEF
# TO JESUS' POWER

*"Is it easier to say 'Your sins are forgiven,' or 'Stand up and walk'? So I will prove to you that the Son of Man has the authority on earth to forgive sins." Then Jesus turned to the paralyzed man and said, "Stand up, pick up your mat, and go home!" And immediately, as everyone watched, the man jumped up, picked up his mat, and went home praising God.*

LUKE 5:23-25 NLT

In this story, Jesus forgave the paralyzed man's sins. This was an invisible miracle—it had no perceivable effect. Yet for Jesus, this was as easy as healing the man's physical malady, which He later did just to prove to the Pharisees and other onlookers that He had the power to do both.

This divine act that Jesus performed on the paralytic is one that He performs on you. When you ask Jesus to pardon your sins and you believe He has done so, you may not see any physical results. But it's a miracle just the same—one whose effects are felt within.

So, the next time you ask Jesus for forgiveness, add your belief to His divine power. . .and experience the miraculous effect of His pardon.

*Thank You, Lord, for forgiving my sins.*
*Help me add my belief to Your power!*

---

## PRAYER JAR INSPIRATION:

*My Jesus works miracles within and without!*

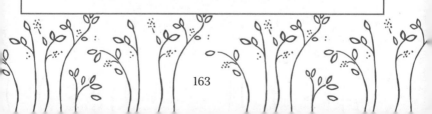

163

# SIN—A CATALYST TO CATASTROPHE

*"This is what the Lord says: Because of what you have done,
I will cause your own household to rebel against you. I will give
your wives to another man before your very eyes, and he will
go to bed with them in public view. You did it secretly, but I will
make this happen to you openly in the sight of all Israel."*

2 SAMUEL 12:11-12 NLT

When David impregnated a married woman (Bathsheba) and then had her husband (Uriah) killed, he did eventually come clean with God. And God did forgive him. But doing so didn't erase the consequences of David's sins. For after David married Bathsheba, their first child died. Then, David's family conflicts careened out of control.

These accounts remind us that forgiveness is great. . .but it's even better not to sin in the first place! Our missteps can set off a potentially lethal avalanche of misfortune that affects everyone in our circle.

Remembering this may prevent you from having to ask for forgiveness at all.

*Lord, help me set my intent each day on following Your
way, knowing that even if I'm later forgiven for veering off
course, my missteps may trip up others in my life.*

## PRAYER JAR INSPIRATION:

*My safest place to be is in God's will and way!*

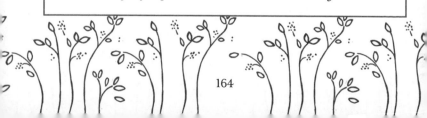

# REAPING AND SOWING

*Those who live only to satisfy their own sinful nature will harvest decay and death from that sinful nature. But those who live to please the Spirit will harvest everlasting life from the Spirit.*

GALATIANS 6:8 NLT

David's third son, Absalom, had a beautiful sister named Tamar. Tamar captured the eye of her half-brother Amnon, David's firstborn son. He was literally sick with desire for his virginal half-sister (2 Samuel 13:1-2).

So Amnon, with the help of a friend, came up with a plan to lure Tamar into Amnon's room. Tamar fell for the ploy and entered Amnon's bedroom, where he overpowered and raped her. Once he was finished with her, his hatred of Tamar grew, and he ordered her out of his sight.

Deeply ashamed, Tamar went into mourning. . .and her brother Absalom began planning his revenge. News of Amnon's atrocity angered David. But he did nothing to punish his firstborn. Perhaps David saw his own failures—his own lust and deception—as all too similar to Amnon's. Regardless of what David thought, his own sin had already set the ball of misdeeds rolling.

When might your own missteps have fostered those of your own family or friends?

*I thank You, Lord, for granting me forgiveness, but I pray that I would always remember this truth: what I sow today, I will reap tomorrow.*

## PRAYER JAR INSPIRATION:

*Each day, Lord, remind me to live to please the Spirit.*

# GOD, THE SCORE SETTLER

*Absalom had begun to make plans for revenge. So Tamar remained a*
*broken woman living in her brother Absalom's house. . . . For his part,*
*Absalom would not talk to Amnon, either nicely or angrily; Absalom*
*hated Amnon for raping his sister Tamar, but he waited patiently.*

2 SAMUEL 13:20, 22 VOICE

After being raped then rejected, Tamar was in a desperate state. In
her culture, marriage would've been out of the question. She would
spend the rest of her years in shame, living in her brother Absalom's
house. Meanwhile, Absalom began to plot his revenge.

Absalom's malice toward his brother Amnon simmered just beneath
the surface. For two years he maintained his facade, neither raging
at nor being friendly with Amnon. But his bitter lack of forgiveness
fermented within him. And then he saw his opportunity to kill Amnon,
whose "fate [was] certain since the day he raped his sister Tamar, for
Absalom [knew] that he would repay Amnon for his terrible deed"
(2 Samuel 13:32 VOICE).

There are some misdeeds that seem unforgivable. Yet, still we are
called to pardon the transgressors—and failing to do so will only lead
to further sin, death, and mayhem. Any retribution is for God to deal
with (Romans 12:19).

> *Give me the strength and desire, Lord, to forgive all*
> *transgressions—no matter how egregious.*

## PRAYER JAR INSPIRATION:

*I look to You, Lord, to settle all scores.*

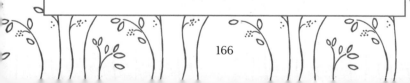

# SINFUL SEPARATION

*We must all die; we are like water spilled on the ground, which cannot be gathered up again. And God does not take away life, but devises means so that he who is banished may not be an utter outcast from Him.*

2 SAMUEL 14:14 AMPC

After killing his brother Amnon, Absalom ran for sanctuary to his maternal grandfather's house. Meanwhile, his father David mourned not only for the death of his son Amnon but for his now-absent son Absalom.

To help David work through this muddle in his mind and heart, his nephew Joab brought a wise woman to talk to him. She presented a fictional scenario that paralleled David's. In her wisdom, she reminded him—and us—that we are all God's banished ones. Our sins keep us from drawing close to God. And in a sense, our banishment is self-inflicted. We have inflicted evil upon others and now run from God's love and forgiveness, ashamed of what we have wrought. We banish God from our minds and hearts.

May we, like the Prodigal Son, pull ourselves together and run to God, begging His pardon. For He is still eager to meet us with open arms and embrace us with His forgiveness.

*Lord, I come running to Your open arms.*

## PRAYER JAR INSPIRATION:

*Lord, help me pull myself together and seek Your forgiveness and presence once more!*

# A NEW HEART AND SPIRIT

*I will judge each of you according to what you have done. Repent!*
*Turn from your wicked ways so that your sins do not trip you up!*
*Get rid of all your wicked ways! Acquire a new heart and a new spirit!*

EZEKIEL 18:30-31 VOICE

Eventually, King David "kissed Absalom and welcomed him back into his good graces" (2 Samuel 14:33 VOICE). The only problem was that, although he'd been forgiven, Absalom hadn't changed. He soon implemented a plan to lead a rebellion against his father. His habit of lying and deceiving others—his lust for power and his love of self—eventually led to Absalom's downfall.

The lesson here is that God does indeed forgive us. . .yet there will still be consequences for the events we set in motion. In addition, we must be *truly* repentant of our misdeeds—after all, God cannot be mocked.

Today, consider some of the times you may have asked for God's forgiveness but not really repented of your sins. Ask God to be gentle with you, to extend to you His mercy and His ever-loving patience and to help you acquire a new heart and a new spirit.

*Lord, help me straighten myself out so that I truly change,*
*turning from my old ways and turning back to Yours.*

> ## PRAYER JAR INSPIRATION:
> *Lord, give me a new heart and spirit!*

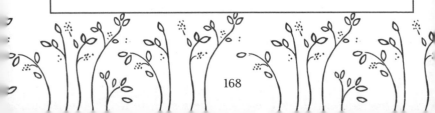

# SILENCE AND SUBMISSION

*The Anointed One suffered for us and left us His example so
that we could follow in His steps. When He was verbally abused,
He didn't return the abuse; when He suffered, He didn't make
threats to cause suffering in return; instead, He trusted that all
would be put right by the One who is just when He judges.*

1 PETER 2:22–23 VOICE

King David had restored his relationship with Absalom, but his son
hadn't changed. And as Absalom's rebellion took hold, David found
himself leaving his throne to flee into the wilderness with the faithful
few who remained with him.

As they traveled, one of King Saul's relatives, Shimei, shouted
hurtful words at David, telling him that his misfortune was God's
punishment on David for having taken Saul's throne and killing his
loyal subjects.

David took Shimei's insults patiently, leaving the man's words in
God's hands, trusting He knew what He was doing.

There will be times when you'll need to avoid taking to heart the
disparaging words and actions of others. Instead, simply leave them in
God's hands, having faith that He will put things right. How might
you apply this concept today?

*Help me, Lord, to leave others' insults in Your hands,
knowing that—in the end—You will make things right.*

## PRAYER JAR INSPIRATION:

*God makes all right.*

# FIRST THING: PRAY

*David and all of those who went into exile with him covered their heads; and weeping, they climbed the Mount of Olives out of the city, David climbing barefoot. Someone told David that his wise counselor Ahithophel was conspiring with Absalom. So David prayed.*

2 Samuel 15:30–31 voice

David had repented of his own deceptions and lust and had been forgiven by God, but the consequences of his actions continued. Now, he'd been ousted from his own throne by Absalom, his son.

As David and his faithful followers continued journeying shoeless into exile, weeping along the way, David learned that his advisor Ahithophel had defected to Absalom's side.

Perhaps this move was God's will. But such news about an old friend and counselor must have wounded David to the heart. So, he did what he could in the moment: he prayed.

Philippians 4:6 (voice) tells us that's *exactly* what we should do: "Don't be anxious about things; instead, pray. Pray about everything. He longs to hear your requests, so talk to God about your needs and be thankful for what has come."

Before you do anything, pray. Tell God what's happening in your life. Ask Him for whatever you need. And He will not only give you His unsurpassable peace but lead you where He would have you go.

*Hear my prayer, Lord.*

## PRAYER JAR INSPIRATION:

*Pray, pray, pray. And I'll find peace, peace, peace.*

# FORGIVE AND FORGET

*Shimei (son of Gera, the Benjaminite from Bahurim), who*
*had abused David on his way into exile, was one of those in*
*the throngs hurrying to meet David. . . . Shimei, the son of*
*Gera, fell in front of the king before he crossed the Jordan.*

2 SAMUEL 19:16, 18 VOICE

After Absalom was killed and his rebellion crushed, David's kingdom was restored. As David prepared to cross the Jordan, Shimei, the man who'd cursed David during Absalom's rebellion, saw which way the wind was blowing and decided to prostrate himself in front of the king.

Shimei said to David, "Please, my lord, don't hold me guilty or hold a grudge for what I did against you on the day you left Jerusalem, cursing you and throwing stones at you. May the king forget it ever happened! I, your servant, know that what I did was wrong" (2 Samuel 19:19-20 VOICE).

Abishai, one of David's nephews and military leaders, thought Shimei should be executed. But David, out of the goodness of his heart, decided to repay Shimei's evil with good—so he forgave the man on the spot, thus reconciling Shimei to him.

David did as Jesus asks: he forgave, choosing to love the other as himself. To whom might you need to extend that same forgiveness?

*Prompt my mind, Spirit. Whom might I need*
*to forgive and what misstep forget?*

## PRAYER JAR INSPIRATION:
*The Lord uses the goodness He planted within*
*me to help me forgive and forget.*

# FORGIVING OURSELVES

Many Bible verses tell of God's promise to forgive us for our misdeeds, but we often have trouble forgiving ourselves. How can we if we are consumed with guilt?

Some people are overcome with so much guilt that they think God could never forgive them. They're convinced that their sins are just too great in quantity or severity. But 1 John 1:9 (KJV) says: "If we confess our sins, he is faithful and just to forgive us our sins, and to cleanse us from all unrighteousness." It's not a question of whether *God* will forgive us but whether *we* will confess our sins. Knowing God forgives us, we must forgive ourselves.

Frequently, those who can't forgive themselves find it easy to forgive others. So, imagine how God must feel when we keep bringing up the same sins He's already taken care of. Jesus told us to come daily to Him for cleansing when He said, "Give us this day our daily bread. And forgive us our debts, as we forgive our debtors" (Matthew 6:11-12 KJV). We should keep short accounts with God and confess our sins every day. . .but not the same ones over and over. Repeatedly asking to be forgiven for the same sins is a clue that you're not forgiving yourself. If you claim God's promise that He will forgive you, then you must forgive yourself.

# GUILT-FREE ZONE

*"Woman, where are they? Does no one condemn*
*you?" "No one, Master." "Neither do I," said Jesus.*
*"Go on your way. From now on, don't sin."*

JOHN 8:10-11 MSG

The scribes and Pharisees had brought an adulteress to Jesus, telling Him she'd been caught in the act. They knew the law required her to be stoned to death. So, hoping to gain evidence with which to accuse Jesus, they asked Him what *He* thought should happen to her.

When Jesus said, "The sinless one among you, go first: Throw the stone" (John 8:7 MSG), the accusers walked away one by one, leaving Jesus alone with the adulteress. That's when He asked her who was left to condemn her. "No one," she responded. Jesus then told her to go her way and sin no more.

Sometimes, the severity of our sin cuts us to the quick, especially when we think of how merciful and kind Jesus is to us who are unworthy. Yet, holding on to that guilt and allowing that black cloud to continually follow us is not how Christ wants us to live. For there's no condemnation for those in Christ Jesus (Romans 8:1-2).

What guilt do you need to let go of today?

*Jesus, I'm so sore from continually kicking myself*
*when You've already freed me from my confessed sin.*
*Help me forgive myself as You've forgiven me.*

# PRAYER JAR INSPIRATION:

*Because of Jesus, I live in a guilt-free zone.*

# SWEPT-AWAY SIN

*I have swept away your wrongdoing, as wind sweeps a cloud*
*from the sky: I have cleared you of your sins, as the sun clears*
*the morning mist. I have rescued you; come back to Me.*
ISAIAH 44:22 VOICE

Whatever wrong you have committed, whatever you did when walking out of the Way, whatever you have confessed to Jesus, He has forgiven you. He has swept your sin away. It no longer hovers over you like a dark cloud, weighing down your otherwise free soul.

Jesus has cleared the air between you and God. He has rescued you from the trap into which you had fallen. It's time for you to feel peace in His presence once more.

Yet, you may have the habit of rehearsing your wrongs, wondering how you might've prevented them and what you can do to avoid them in the future. You keep hanging on to the guilt, having been forgiven by God but not by yourself.

Whatever dark cloud has been following you, lift it up to Jesus today. Allow His love to banish it from your presence. Let His light shine through you once more.

There's nothing you can do that Jesus can't forgive. Isn't it time you forgave yourself?

*Thank You, Lord, for sweeping my sin away. Help me breathe*
*easy once more, allowing my guilt to dissipate in Your light.*

## PRAYER JAR INSPIRATION:

*Jesus, Your light guides me back into Your presence.*

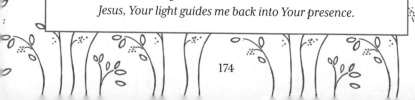

# FORGET ABOUT IT

*This is what GOD says, the GOD who builds a road right through the*
*ocean, who carves a path through pounding waves. . . . "Forget about*
*what's happened; don't keep going over old history. Be alert, be present.*
*I'm about to do something brand-new. It's bursting out! Don't you see it?*
*There it is! I'm making a road through the desert, rivers in the badlands."*

ISAIAH 43:16, 18-19 MSG

Instead of focusing on confessed and forgiven sins, why not focus on what God is doing in your life, your family, and your world right now?

Perhaps you keep mentally flashing back to your misdeed. You keep your head down, glaring at the misstep you've made and wondering if it'll happen again. You've prayed and prayed about it, but moving on still feels impossible.

God tells you to let go! He has! Ages ago! So, start looking up instead of down. With a sense of expectancy, watch for what God's preparing to do. He's making a new road—just for you! He's cutting a path through the desert, a river through the wilderness. Can you see it?

*Lord, help me to keep my eyes on You, to stop looking back at*
*things I cannot change. Show me something new in my life!*

---

## PRAYER JAR INSPIRATION:

*God, You've forgotten the past. Help me do the same.*
*Open my eyes to the new way You're making before me!*

---

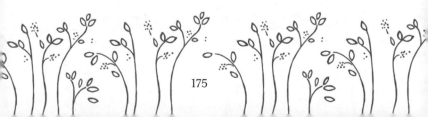

# PAYING THE CONSEQUENCES

*Look on me with a heart of mercy, O God, according to*
*Your generous love. According to Your great compassion,*
*wipe out every consequence of my shameful crimes.*

PSALM 51:1 VOICE

After David slept with and impregnated the married Bathsheba, he arranged things so that her husband Uriah would be killed in battle. David tried to hide his misdeeds from God, but he later confessed and repented of them. Although God forgave David's sins, the prophet Nathan told him, "Because you scorned the Lord by these acts, giving His enemies reason to mock Him, the child you conceived in deceit will die" (2 Samuel 12:14 VOICE).

Yet, David still hoped God might change His mind. So he remained prostrate on the ground, fasting and praying, hoping for God's mercy to fall upon his child. When David and Bathsheba's son died, David rose, washed, changed his clothes, and worshiped God. Then, he came home and ate, knowing he could not bring his baby back in his own power—but that one day, they would be together again in heaven.

Later, God blessed David and Bathsheba with another son whom they named Jedidiah (a.k.a. Solomon), meaning "beloved of the Lord."

We can't change the consequences of our sins, but we can know that the God who forgives will once again bless.

*Although I cannot change the consequences of my*
*actions, Lord, I know You will bless me once more.*

## PRAYER JAR INSPIRATION:
*Praise God for His forgiveness and grace!*

# GUILT FACE-OFF

*Cleanse me from my sins. For I am fully aware of all I have done
wrong, and my guilt is there, staring me in the face. It was against
You, only You, that I sinned, for I have done what You say is
wrong, right before Your eyes. So when You speak, You are in the
right. When You judge, Your judgments are pure and true.*

PSALM 51:2-4 VOICE

You've already told God when, where, why, and how you've messed up.
You've told Him what you've done and to whom. You've told Him that
you're sorry for your words, thoughts, and deeds—that you'll endeavor
to never walk that dark road again. You've asked God to cleanse you
for your sins, knowing that it was really Him whom you'd injured.
You understand that God has forgiven you. Yet still, to this day, in
this moment, your guilt is sitting right there, staring you in the face.

Move on, woman of the Way! You've been forgiven by *God*! Turn
your face from the darkness of your guilt, then turn full face into God's
light. For in Christ you are free, free indeed!

*Today, Lord, I turn my face from the darkness and stare
into Your light. Take my hand! Lead me on!*

---

# PRAYER JAR INSPIRATION:

*I am free, lifted up, into God's light!*

---

# KEEP MOVING FORWARD

*I was guilty from the day I was born, a sinner from the time my
mother became pregnant with me. But still, You long to enthrone
truth throughout my being; in unseen places deep within me,
You show me wisdom. Cleanse me of my wickedness with hyssop,
and I will be clean. If You wash me, I will be whiter than snow.*

PSALM 51:5-7 VOICE

We've all been born into sin. But when we meet Jesus—when we begin
to have faith in Him and attempt to walk His way—we become new
beings within. We spend our time looking not at fame and fortune but
at God's Word. For His promises and wisdom help us stay on the right
road, bringing His light to the dark and unseen places deep within us.

Yes, you may have sinned. And chances are, it won't be the last
time. But know that Jesus can and will pick you up each time you
fall. He will brush you off, remove the tiny stones embedded in your
palms, wash your scraped knees, retie your shoelaces, and set you on
your feet again. No need to keep looking back at the place you tripped.
Keep moving forward, hand in hand with Jesus.

*Thanks for cleaning me up from the fall I took, Lord.
Hold my hand as I move forward with You.*

## PRAYER JAR INSPIRATION:

*With Jesus by my side, I can (and will) walk on!*

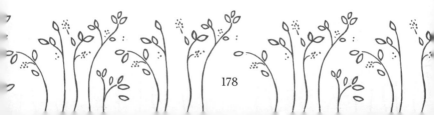

# A FRESH START

*Tune me in to foot-tapping songs, set these once-broken bones to dancing. Don't look too close for blemishes, give me a clean bill of health. God, make a fresh start in me, shape a Genesis week from the chaos of my life. Don't throw me out with the trash, or fail to breathe holiness in me. Bring me back from gray exile, put a fresh wind in my sails!*

PSALM 51:8–12 MSG

Now that you've been forgiven by God and Jesus has cleaned you up, it's time to celebrate! Turn on some praise music and start singing at the top of your voice. It doesn't matter if you're tone deaf or can't sing vibrato. Just sing! All praise is good music to God's ears.

Hopefully, by this time, you've forgiven yourself and are ready to move on. If so, ask God to make a fresh start within you, to have His Spirit hover over the chaos in your life and speak some light into it. Ask the Lord to forget your sins and to remove all guilt from your heart and soul. When you do, He'll pull you close, give you a big hug of love, and gently prod you forward.

But it's up to *you* to take the first steps.

*Thank You, Lord, for giving me a new start!*
*With Your light, I will find my way!*

---

## PRAYER JAR INSPIRATION:

*The Spirit hovers over me and speaks, "Light!" into my chaos!*

---

# TRUE OFFERING

*I would surrender my dearest possessions or destroy all*
*that I prize to prove my regret, but You don't take pleasure*
*in sacrifices or burnt offerings. What sacrifice I can offer*
*You is my broken spirit because a broken spirit, O God,*
*a heart that honestly regrets the past, You won't detest.*

<small>PSALM 51:16-17 VOICE</small>

So you messed up big time. Hopefully, you truly regret the damage
that your misstep caused. You feel remorse deep within your heart.
You know you've displeased God, and now you want to earnestly
show Him that remorse.

You could walk around for days with a downcast air. You might
even want to surrender some prized possession so that God will see
how deep your regret truly is. But there's no need! God doesn't want
you to walk around with your head down or to give up your favorite
food, book, or activity. The best way to show your deep and sincere
remorse is to come to Him with a broken spirit. A sore heart. A soulful
regret. That kind of offering He will not despise.

*Lord, I lift up to You a heart that's sore and a spirit that's crushed*
*because of what I have done. They're Yours for the taking.*

## PRAYER JAR INSPIRATION:

*Thank You, Lord, for accepting the offer of my sincere remorse.*

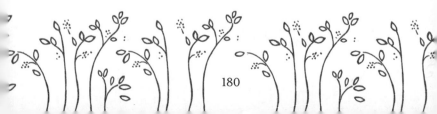

# FAITH TESTERS

*Consider it a sheer gift, friends, when tests and challenges come at you from all sides. You know that under pressure, your faith-life is forced into the open and shows its true colors. So don't try to get out of anything prematurely. Let it do its work so you become mature and well-developed, not deficient in any way.*

JAMES 1:2-4 MSG

When Judas and his cohorts came to arrest Jesus, Peter not only fled with the others but, when accused of knowing Him, ended up denying Jesus three times! His faith was tested in a major way. And yet, Jesus still forgave him. In fact, He asked Peter three times if he loved Him. All three times, Peter said yes, and Jesus responded by saying, "Take care of My lambs. . . . Shepherd My sheep. . . . Look after My sheep" (John 21:15-17 VOICE).

Peter's challenges made his faith stronger. He became a disciple who was eager and more than able to lead the flock of new believers who would come to know Jesus as he did.

Challenges and tests will make you stronger. So, forgive yourself for your failures as Jesus has forgiven you. This will allow your faith life to grow higher as you live more for Jesus.

*Jesus, may my trials work to strengthen my faith in You!*

## PRAYER JAR INSPIRATION:
*May my challenges work to increase my faith in Jesus!*

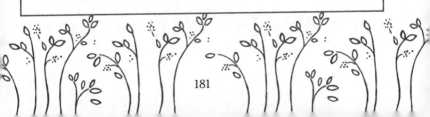

# TIME AFTER TIME

*Peter came up to Him and said, "Lord, how many times may*
*my brother sin against me and I forgive him and let it go?*
*[As many as] up to seven times?" Jesus answered him, "I tell*
*you, not up to seven times, but seventy times seven!"*

MATTHEW 18:21-22 AMPC

So, you've made a mistake. And you feel miserable about it. You truly regret your actions and how much you may have hurt someone. Perhaps that "someone" was your husband or fiancé. One of your parents or a sibling. Your boss or teacher.

Or, even worse, perhaps you injured a child with your words. You didn't mean to say what you said—the words just flew out. You witnessed the harm they caused this young, innocent child, and you feel horrible that you cannot take them back. You begin to wonder if you've damaged him for life!

So, you go to God. You've shown true repentance. You've asked for His forgiveness. Yet, the scene of your mishap keeps playing over and over in your mind.

Just as you are to forgive others "seventy times seven," you must do so for yourself. Whenever the scene of your slipup shows up, forgive yourself, knowing God has already moved on. Isn't it time you did the same?

*Lord, help me forgive myself so that I can let*
*remorse go and move forward with You.*

## PRAYER JAR INSPIRATION:

*God, help me learn to forgive myself.*

# LETTING GO

*Whenever you stand praying, if you have anything against*
*anyone, forgive him and let it drop (leave it, let it go), in order*
*that your Father Who is in heaven may also forgive you your*
*[own] failings and shortcomings and let them drop.*

MARK 11:25 AMPC

When you are praying to God—whether you're sitting, standing, kneeling, or lying down—Jesus tells you to let go of any resentment you have against anyone. Why? So that your Father God in heaven will forgive and let go of all the wrongs *you've* done.

The same holds true if you've yet to forgive yourself. If the movie screen of your mind is stuck on the scene of your transgression, it will deepen whatever groove of remorse still resides within your heart. Soon, you'll be down so deep that you'll have trouble seeing any of God's light in your life.

Right now, go before God in prayer and let go of any remorse or bitterness you're still harboring against yourself. Drop it into God's light and watch it dissolve. Learn to forgive yourself, just like you forgive others.

*Lord, in the light of Your power and mercy, I release the unforgiveness*
*I've been harboring deep within me. In Jesus' name, amen.*

## PRAYER JAR INSPIRATION:

*I forgive myself, just as Father God forgives me.*

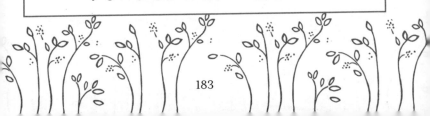

# FORGIVING QUICKLY
# AND THOROUGHLY

*Make a clean break with all cutting, backbiting, profane talk.*
*Be gentle with one another, sensitive. Forgive one another as*
*quickly and thoroughly as God in Christ forgave you.*

EPHESIANS 4:31-32 MSG

As soon as you confess your mistake to God, as soon as your sincere regret reaches the Father's heart, as soon as you ask His forgiveness, He has already thoroughly forgiven you. It's a done deal!

Yet, sometimes it may seem impossible to forgive yourself. On those days, your mental chatter becomes harmful. That inner voice starts cutting you down, treating you harshly.

Get it into your head that God has forgiven you for *all* you've done. It's time to forgive yourself. If that proves to be difficult, ask God for assistance. Ask Him to fill your mind with His good Word, to remind you that you are loved. Allow His hand of healing to touch your heart. See His eyes of love looking into yours. Tell yourself it's okay, that you have God's permission to forgive yourself just as quickly and thoroughly as He has forgiven you.

*Thank You, Lord, for helping me forgive myself.*

## PRAYER JAR INSPIRATION:

*I pledge to forgive myself and others as quickly*
*and thoroughly as God forgives me!*

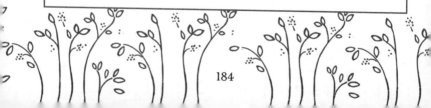

# POWER OF FORGIVENESS

God's power of forgiveness was released into the world by the prayer Jesus spoke as He hung on the cross: "Father, forgive them; for they know not what they do" (Luke 23:34 KJV). He understood that those who crucified Him were fulfilling God's plan of salvation for everyone who would believe in Him as the Son of God. For such forgiveness to be possible, there had to be a perfect living sacrifice.

There are three things that reveal the depth of our relationship with God: (1) The way we love people, (2) the way we accept people, and (3) the way we forgive people. When we refuse to forgive others, we put them—and ourselves—in bondage to our unforgiveness. Emotional wounds are hard to heal, but when we refuse to think those thoughts anymore and decide to follow the Bible's prescription, freedom from an unforgiving spirit will be ours.

We can learn the power of forgiveness only by doing it. . .and no one can do it for us. Jesus forgives us, so we must forgive ourselves and others.

# THE SAME GOD

*I am your brother, Joseph, whom you sold into Egypt. . . .*
*God sent me here ahead of you to make sure you and your*
*families survive this terrible ordeal and have a remnant left on*
*earth. So it wasn't really you who sent me here, but God; the*
*same God who made me an advisor to Pharaoh, master of his*
*household, and ruler over everyone in the land of Egypt.*

<small>GENESIS 45:4, 7-8 VOICE</small>

God had given Joseph a dream—actually *two* dreams—that one day his brothers would bow down to him. Joseph held on to that dream and his God even when he was sold by his brothers to some traders, was made a slave to an Egyptian captain of the palace guards, was accused of rape, and was imprisoned and left forgotten in the dungeon.

Because Joseph was more focused on God's goodness than on the wickedness of his tormentors, he prospered no matter where he went. His forgiveness, his focus on God, and his obedience to Him allowed God to work His dream through this man.

There is power in forgiveness. Have you found yours?

*Lord, You are with me through everything. May that knowledge*
*help me tap into the power of Your forgiveness!*

---

## PRAYER JAR INSPIRATION:

*When I forgive, I can move forward with God.*

---

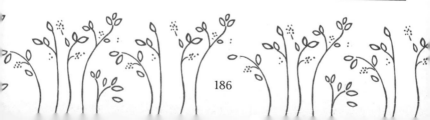

186

# REGARDLESS OF TREATMENT

*That night Paul had a vision: A man from Macedonia in northern Greece was standing there, pleading with him, "Come over to Macedonia and help us!" So we decided to leave for Macedonia at once, having concluded that God was calling us to preach the Good News there.*

ACTS 16:9-10 NLT

Prompted by God, Paul and Silas left with others to Macedonia. One day, while they were heading to a place of prayer, a slave girl who worked as a fortune teller for her owners kept following them around. She'd shout, "These men are servants of the Most High God, and they have come to tell you how to be saved" (Acts 16:17 NLT).

This happened day after day until Paul, exasperated with her, commanded in the name of Jesus Christ that the demon within her come out. And it did! This, however, left her owners without their source of income. So they dragged Paul and Silas before the authorities and shouted accusations against them. A mob soon formed. The city officials ordered Paul and Silas to be severely beaten with rods and then chained up in prison. Despite their treatment, Paul and Silas spent the night praying and singing praises to God.

No matter what situation we find ourselves in, we can forgive those who persecute us and continue to worship the One who is for us.

*Lord, help me forgive others no matter what treatment I receive at their hands.*

## PRAYER JAR INSPIRATION:

*May I continue to follow my dream as I walk with my God.*

# SHAKEN TO THE FOUNDATIONS

*Around midnight Paul and Silas were praying and singing hymns to God, and the other prisoners were listening. Suddenly, there was a massive earthquake, and the prison was shaken to its foundations. All the doors immediately flew open, and the chains of every prisoner fell off!*

ACTS 16:25-26 NLT

Because Paul and Silas had decided to keep their hearts, eyes, spirits, minds, and souls attuned to God and His plans, they were able to pray and praise God in the worst of conditions.

They had been arrested, beaten, thrown into a prison cell, and chained. Yet, because they were attuned to God instead of the tragedy of their circumstance, God used His amazing power to shake the prison to its foundations. The cell doors flew open and every prisoner's chains fell off! They were free! Yet, even then, they didn't leave.

When the jailer woke to see the doors open, he figured the prisoners had escaped and he'd be blamed. Just as he was about to kill himself with his sword, Paul stopped him, letting him know all were present and accounted for.

God's power comes with your forgiveness!

*Lord, remind me each day of the power that comes when I forgive others. . .and when You forgive me!*

## PRAYER JAR INSPIRATION:

*God's power is unleashed when I forgive others!*

# BELIEVE AND BE SAVED

*The jailer called for lights and ran to the dungeon and fell
down trembling before Paul and Silas. Then he brought them
out and asked, "Sirs, what must I do to be saved?" They
replied, "Believe in the Lord Jesus and you will be saved."*

ACTS 16:29-31 NLT

The prison doors had flown open. The prisoners' chains had fallen off!
And still they remained under the jailer's care.

Paul and Silas could've run off and escaped. But instead, their hearts
lurched at the idea that their jailer (the one who'd put them behind
bars and now thought he'd lost his charges) might kill himself. So, they
told him to put his sword down, reassuring him they were still there.

The believers' words and actions showed the jailer what he'd been
missing. He wanted to become like them, so he asked how he could
be saved. They said all he had to do was believe.

Those words apply to us today. We say we believe, yet we continue
to nurse our resentments and bitterness toward others. In so doing,
we don't reflect the light of Jesus.

Today, make a commitment to yourself and God to forgive as He
forgives you—and to simply believe that He will make all things right
in the end, changing you and everyone else!

*Help me, Lord, to forgive as You forgive. Help me
to let go of all resentments and bitterness.*

## PRAYER JAR INSPIRATION:

*Believing Jesus has a better way will save me!*

189

# GOD'S GOODNESS

*"Men," he said, "I believe there is trouble ahead if we go on—shipwreck, loss of cargo, and danger to our lives as well." But the officer in charge of the prisoners listened more to the ship's captain and the owner than to Paul.*

ACTS 27:10-11 NLT

Have you ever given advice to others and they turned away from it, much to the detriment of everyone involved? That's what happened to the apostle Paul.

Paul and other prisoners were aboard a ship bound for Rome. When the weather became dangerous for sea travel, Paul advised that they stay at the town of Fair Havens. But the officer ignored his counsel, and they went on. Sure enough, they soon ran into big trouble. Yet, instead of nursing a grudge, Paul not only forgave but encouraged his fellow shipmates, saying, "Take courage! None of you will lose your lives, even though the ship will go down. For last night an angel of the God to whom I belong and whom I serve stood beside me, and he said, 'Don't be afraid, Paul, for you will surely stand trial before Caesar! What's more, God in his goodness has granted safety to everyone sailing with you'" (Acts 27:22-24 NLT).

No matter how often people might ignore your advice, forgive and forget. For God in His goodness always stands beside you.

*Thank You, Lord, for Your goodness.*

## PRAYER JAR INSPIRATION:
*God stands by my side!*

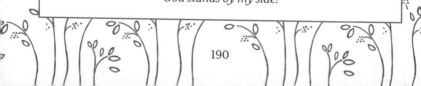

# COMPLETE CONFIDENCE

*So keep up your courage, men, for I have faith (complete confidence) in God that it will be exactly as it was told me; but we shall have to be stranded on some island.*

ACTS 27:25-26 AMPC

The men aboard the ship hadn't listened to Paul's advice the first time around when he'd told them it wasn't safe to leave Fair Havens. But he didn't hold a grudge. Instead, he just moved on with his life, continuing to listen to God and follow His lead. Thus, the next time Paul offered his advice—telling them they should take courage because God had told him that they'd all live through this seafaring adventure—they believed him. For Paul had demonstrated to them the complete confidence he had in his God!

Later, Paul advised against letting some sailors escape, warning them, "Unless these men remain in the ship, you cannot be saved" (Acts 27:31 AMPC). And when Paul encouraged them to eat for their own safety, telling them it would give them strength, they ate and became more cheerful (Acts 27:33-36). In the end, all 276 souls on the ship made it safely to land.

Understand the power of God's forgiveness. Believe He means what He says. And from that belief, you'll find courage—the complete confidence to forgive and encourage all!

*Thank You, Lord, for giving me the faith and courage to forgive.*

## PRAYER JAR INSPIRATION:

*My complete confidence is in my God!*

# MAKING THINGS RIGHT

*"If you enter your place of worship and, about to make an offering,
you suddenly remember a grudge a friend has against you, abandon
your offering, leave immediately, go to this friend and make things
right. Then and only then, come back and work things out with God."*

MATTHEW 5:23-24 MSG

The power of forgiveness goes both ways: there's power in your
forgiving others, *and* there's power in others forgiving you. If you
want peace of mind, if you want to get closer to God, if you want to
experience the purity and power of love, you must make things right
with anyone you've offended.

This might mean humbling yourself before the person you've hurt.
It may entail confessing a fault that sometimes gets you into hot water
with others. It may even mean apologizing to the offended party.
Whatever this clearing of the air requires, do it sincerely and to the
best of your ability. Do it knowing that Jesus requires you not just to
love Him but to love others as yourself. Do it today without delay.

*Lord, give me the courage and the humbleness to make
things right with those I've offended. Help me offer my
love and apology whenever they're needed.*

## PRAYER JAR INSPIRATION:

*Jesus makes all things right.*

# DOUBLE BLESSINGS

*After Job had prayed for his friends, the Lord restored his prosperity and doubled his previous possessions. . . . So the Lord blessed the last part of Job's life more than the first. . . . Job lived 140 years after this and saw his children and their children to the fourth generation. Then Job died, old and full of days.*

JOB 42:10, 12, 16-17 HCSB

The last chapter of Job begins with Job's apology to the Lord, which ends with the words "I take back everything I said, and I sit in dust and ashes to show my repentance" (Job 42:6 NLT).

After Job had made things right with God, God took Job's side against his "friends," who'd presented an inaccurate picture of Him to Job. God ordered them to make a sacrifice to Him. Then He told them, "My servant Job will pray for you, and I will accept his prayer on your behalf. I will not treat you as you deserve" (Job 42:8 NLT).

It appears that Job himself was not fully forgiven by God until he had prayed for his friends with a loving and sincere heart! Once he had done so, God not only restored what Job had lost but doubled his blessings.

Woman of the Way, live with love and forgiveness, knowing that when you do, God will doubly bless you.

*Thank You, God, for all Your love, forgiveness, and blessings.*

## PRAYER JAR INSPIRATION:

*There's eternal power in love and forgiveness!*

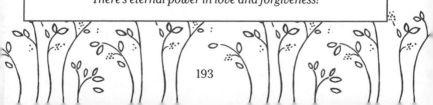

# GRACE, LOVE, AND MERCY AMID FORGIVENESS

Without forgiveness, it's impossible to achieve grace, love, or mercy. When you do not forgive, you are harboring negative emotions toward those who have harmed you.

Grace, mercy, love, and forgiveness all work together. Scripture defines grace as God's unmerited favor. That means God gives us something we could never earn or deserve. Mercy, however, is God not giving us the punishment we *do* deserve.

So, what about love and forgiveness? Scripture commands us to love even as God has loved us. We can't show love without forgiveness, and we can't forgive without love. First Corinthians 13:13 (KJV) sums it up: "And now abideth faith, hope, charity, these three; but the greatest of these is charity." Why is charity (love) that important? Because love forgives.

Everything God is to us can be summed up in one word: grace. As believers, we know that love, mercy, and forgiveness are packed inside the wonderful grace of God.

# MERCY, PLEASE!

*If you're listening, here's My message: Keep loving your enemies
no matter what they do. Keep doing good to those who hate you.
Keep speaking blessings on those who curse you. Keep praying
for those who mistreat you. If someone strikes you on one cheek,
offer the other cheek too. If someone steals your coat, offer him
your shirt too. If someone begs from you, give to him. If someone
robs you of your valuables, don't demand them back.*
LUKE 6:27-30 VOICE

It takes a lot of grace, love, and mercy to live a life that meets Jesus'
standards. For He wants you to love not just those who are easy to
love but those who've wounded you.

Jesus wants you to continue doing good to those who hate you.
To keep speaking blessings into the lives of those who curse you. To
keep praying for those who've abused you.

All that—*plus* offering your cheek to someone who has already
reddened the first one, offering your shirt to someone who has already
taken your coat, giving to beggars, and allowing those who have stolen
something to keep it—is a tall order indeed! But with God's help, it
is possible.

How can you practice extending mercy to others as Jesus extends
it to you?

*Help me, Lord, to live my life with an
abundance of grace, love, and mercy!*

## PRAYER JAR INSPIRATION:

*May I see others, even enemies, through the loving eyes of Christ.*

# ABOVE ALL THINGS

*Above all things have intense and unfailing love for one another, for love covers a multitude of sins [forgives and disregards the offenses of others].*

1 PETER 4:8 AMPC

The apostle Peter made no bones about it: the new believers must realize that they may have to suffer, just as Jesus did. That their lives were to be controlled not by their earthly desires, but by the will of God. That they were to live not as they might have in the past, but to stand apart from the ungodly crowd—to play by the rules of God's game, not of their flesh-satisfying desires.

To that end, Peter tells believers to keep a clear head and pray with all their hearts.

And, above all things, to love one another, forgiving and forgetting the wrongs done against them.

Isn't that what Jesus' message always comes down to? Love. No matter what wrong people have done against you, no matter how much they've pained you, no matter what you suffered at their hands, love. For love forgives and forgets.

Who needs that kind of love from you today? Will you extend it?

*Lord, to live as You call me to live, I need an abundance of Your love! Help me follow Your example. Help me love as You loved.*

## PRAYER JAR INSPIRATION:

*Above all things, I must love as Jesus loved.*

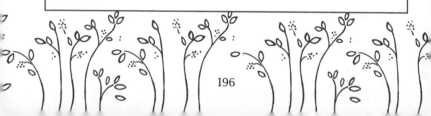

# FORGIVEN MUCH, LOVE MUCH

*This woman has been forgiven much, and she is showing
much love. But the person who has shown little love
shows how little forgiveness he has received.*

LUKE 7:47 VOICE

God's grace, love, and mercy are amazingly powerful forces that, when combined, can transform the most sinful—those with the darkest of hearts, those who could never find a way to right their wrongs—into beings of much love.

Such was the case of the woman of ill repute whom Jesus had forgiven. She came to Him and cried, and then she began using her tears and her hair to clean His feet. But she didn't stop there. She also put her lips to His feet, covering them with her kisses. Then, she poured expensive perfumed oil onto them. Because Jesus had forgiven her plethora of sins, she was overflowing with her love for Him. And it was because of her faith that He could forgive her and set her free from "all the distresses that are experienced as the result of sin" (Luke 7:50 AMPC).

You, too, can experience that freedom that comes from faith, love, and forgiveness. Revel in it today! Love much because you have been forgiven much!

*Lord, may my love for You be abundant,
for You have forgiven me for so much!*

## PRAYER JAR INSPIRATION:

*Because I've been forgiven much, my love for Jesus is
overwhelming—my peace within, overflowing!*

# FORGIVE EVERYONE OF ALL

*As they stoned him, Stephen prayed, "Lord Jesus, receive my*
*spirit." He fell to his knees, shouting, "Lord, don't charge them with*
*this sin!" And with that, he died. Saul was one of the witnesses,*
*and he agreed completely with the killing of Stephen.*

ACTS 7:59–8:1 NLT

Stephen was "a man full of faith and the Holy Spirit" (Acts 6:5 NLT). Due to his abundant grace and power, Stephen performed many wonders and miracles in public. However, a certain group of people, the Free Synagogue, opposed him. But because the Spirit had given Stephen such great wisdom, he always ended up humiliating his opponents. Thus, in an act of revenge, they started a rumor that they'd "heard Stephen speak blasphemies against Moses and God" (Acts 6:11 VOICE). Before he knew it, Stephen had been dragged before the Sanhedrin council.

Stephen's account of Jewish history, which ended with a blistering accusation that the Jewish leaders had killed the Messiah, inflamed the council. He was quickly stoned to death in front of Saul of Tarsus, who would later be blinded on his way to Damascus and become an apostle of Jesus Christ.

God can transform the least likely of people and use them for His purposes. So, tap into His grace, mercy, and love—and forgive everyone of all.

*Today, Lord, I tap into Your love with the intent of forgiving all for all.*

## PRAYER JAR INSPIRATION:

*Lord, use me as Your tool of love and forgiveness.*

# WOMAN AT WORK

*Work at living in peace with everyone, and work at living a
holy life, for those who are not holy will not see the Lord.*

HEBREWS 12:14 NLT

Within today's verse we find echoes of Psalm 34:14 (VOICE), which
tells us to "walk away from the evil things of the world, and always
seek peace and pursue it." That means that to find the peace you
treasure, you're going to need to extend mercy, love, and grace to your
fellow humans.

At the same time, you're to make your own peace with God. That's
where holiness comes in. You must strive to become more and more
like Jesus, to be pure in heart just as He was. For as Matthew 5:8 (MSG)
confirms, "You're blessed when you get your inside world—your mind
and heart—put right. Then you can see God in the outside world."

How would your life change if you extended mercy, love, and grace
to everyone, making it your intent to not only live a life of peace with
them but with God? How about trying that out today?

*Help me, Lord, as I work to live at peace and live a holy life.*

---

## PRAYER JAR INSPIRATION:

*Today, my intent is to live at peace with fellow humans and God!*

---

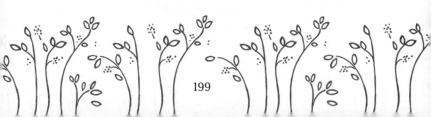

# TEARING DOWN FENCES

*Don't secretly hate your neighbor. If you have something against him, get it out into the open; otherwise you are an accomplice in his guilt. Don't seek revenge or carry a grudge against any of your people. Love your neighbor as yourself. I am God.*

LEVITICUS 19:17-18 MSG

Leviticus 19:13-16 gives some dos and don'ts for getting along with your fellow humans: don't exploit or rob your neighbor; don't insult those who are deaf nor trip those who are blind; don't pervert justice nor judge them unfairly; don't talk about them behind their backs; don't just stand there when they're in danger but help them whenever you can.

Leviticus 19:17-18 gets to the heart of the matter, tying all those verses together: don't hate your neighbor; love him instead. If your neighbor is doing something wrong, talk it out. Get it out in the open. Neither seek revenge nor hold a grudge. Instead, love your neighbor as you love yourself.

Loving your neighbor and seeking the good of others might be difficult, especially in a climate where kindness seems foreign. Yet, you have a Father who can give you all the aid you need in loving those who seem unlovable. Sometimes, all it takes is one act of love and generosity to tear down the strongest of fences.

*Help me love as You love, Lord.*

## PRAYER JAR INSPIRATION:

*May kindness rule my day and heart.*

# UNFORCED RHYTHMS
# OF GRACE

*"Are you tired? Worn out? Burned out on religion? Come to me. Get*
*away with me and you'll recover your life. I'll show you how to take a*
*real rest. Walk with me and work with me—watch how I do it. Learn the*
*unforced rhythms of grace. I won't lay anything heavy or ill-fitting on*
*you. Keep company with me and you'll learn to live freely and lightly."*

MATTHEW 11:28-30 MSG

When you feel empty, tired, and depleted of grace, love, and mercy,
turn to Jesus. Take a rest in Him, allowing Him to refit and refuel
you, to refresh and replenish you. He, your Shepherd, will lead you to
green pastures and quiet streams. There, He will renew your strength—
mentally, emotionally, physically, and spiritually. He will lead you to
the place where you are once again able and eager to forgive those
who've wronged you.

When you feel lost and alone, take a rest with Jesus. He will then
help you rise up once more and learn those unforced rhythms of
grace. Jesus will help you find a way to not only forgive but forget—to
dissolve whatever bitterness lingers in your heart. Hang with Him,
and you'll find the power to live the life for which you were designed.

*I come to You, Lord, ready to hide out for a while,*
*to get a good rest so that I can rise again in You.*

---

# PRAYER JAR INSPIRATION:

*In Jesus, I find the way to walk with grace.*

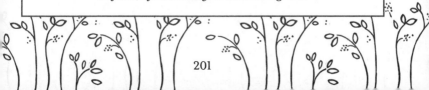

# DARE TO BELIEVE

*Jesus listened to her story.*
***Jesus:*** *Daughter, you are well because you dared*
*to believe. Go in peace, and stay well.*

MARK 5:34 VOICE

Sometimes you may feel like an outcast, even within your own church. Perhaps an inability to forgive lies at the root of that feeling. No matter what you do, you can't seem to let things go.

That's okay. You don't have to travel this road alone. Armed with your faith in the Miracle Man you follow, sneak up behind Him and, no matter the size of the crowd around you, reach out to touch His cloak. As you do so, tell yourself, "Even if all I feel is empty air, I *know* He will give me the love and compassion I need to forgive."

As soon as your fingers feel that spiritual air, your resentment will fade. You will feel whole once again as He removes your pain and injury. At the same time, Jesus will feel the power traveling from Him to you. He will know that you have reached out—that you are well because you dared to believe.

*Thank You, Lord, for the peace, healing, and love*
*I now have. Help me use it to forgive.*

## PRAYER JAR INSPIRATION:
*I dare to believe Jesus.*

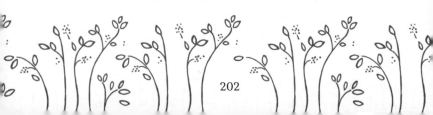

# SCRIPTURE INDEX

## OLD TESTAMENT

# IF YOU LOVED
# THE PRAYER JAR DEVOTIONAL:
# FORGIVENESS. . .

You'll also love bestselling author Wanda E. Brunstetter's
The Prayer Jars Fiction Series

The Hope Jar
978-1-62416-747-8

The Forgiving Jar
978-1-62416-748-5

The Healing Jar
978-1-62416-749-2

Antique jars hidden around an Amish farm are found filled with slips of paper containing thoughts, quotes, and prayers by an unknown author. Three young women each find a jar that takes her on a journey of personal reflection. When the author is revealed, can the jars become a tool to restore a family's lost hopes and faith for the future?